CW00825995

ANGLOPHILE
VIGNETTES

Other books by Jonathan Thomas

Adventures in Anglotopia
Anglotopia's Dictionary of British English

Other Books by Anglotopia

101 London Travel Tips
101 Budget Britain Travel Tips

ANGLOPHILE VIGNETTES

FIFTY LITTLE STORIES ABOUT BRITAIN

BY JONATHAN THOMAS

Copyright © 2020 by Jonathan Thomas

Cover Design by Jonathan Thomas
Cover Images by Jonathan Thomas
Cover Copyright © 2020 Anglotopia LLC

Anglotopia LLC supports the right to free expression and the value of copyright. The
purpose of copyright is to encourage writers and artists to produce the creative works that
enrich our culture.

The scanning, uploading, and distribution of this book without permission is a theft of the
author's intellectual property. If you would like permission to use material from the book
(other than for review purposes), please contact info@anglotopia.net. Thank you for your
support of the author's rights.

Anglotopia Press - An Imprint of Anglotopia LLC
www.anglotopia.press

Printed in the United States of America

First US Edition: December 2020

Published by Anglotopia Press, an imprint of Anglotopia LLC.
The Anglotopia Press Name and Logo is a trademark of Anglotopia LLC.

Print Book interior design by Jonathan Thomas, all fonts used with license.

All photographs © Jonathan Thomas

ISBN: 9781735663920

Dedicated to all lovers of Britain, unable to go there.
We will be back. Until then, this book is for you.

Table of Contents

INTRODUCTION

The book exists because of the Coronavirus. When 'it' started in full swing in early 2020, and we became locked down, I wanted to put out more articles on Anglotopia about Britain that could maybe help people cope with the situation. It would be a long time before any of us could go back to Britain (and of this writing, it's still a no-go zone). Also I didn't have a lot of spare time to write long articles, as I returned to the corporate world in 2020.

Anglophile Vignettes were born. Little stories about Britain. Little scenes from my twenty years of travel in the wonderful country that the United Kingdom gave to us. One technique I learned at a writing workshop a few years ago was to brainstorm and then write short scenes. These would become elements of larger works when the time was right. It was important just to get them written down.

Going through my writing notebook on my computer, I had lots of scenes that still hadn't found a home in other works. Some I'd intended to be in my last book, *Adventures in Anglotopia*, but didn't get used. Others I was just saving for the future. Now seemed as good a time as any.

So this book is a series of scenes. Some are very short, some are quite a bit longer. I have tried to space the long ones out, so you'd have a few short ones, then a long one to break everything up. There are a total of fifty Anglophile Vignettes in this book. About 2/3 of them were originally published on Anglotopia.net.; the rest I've 'saved' for this book and you can't read them anywhere else.

Each little scene or story is like a meditation on something lovely about Britain. Almost like prayers - the prayers that we're all having, hoping that we can all return to the country we love so much as soon as possible. It's still going to be a while. So I want you to have this collection of memories, stories, and experiences to help take you there in your mind until you can go in person.

Happy Future Travels!

Jonathan Thomas
Publisher
Anglotopia

The First Flight

I'm sitting on my deck, my kids are playing in the pool. A jet flies overhead. Then another. And another. I live under a flight path into O'Hare International Airport. Not only that, the planes also begin their descent right above me. They make a lot of noise. I don't mind. Whenever I hear the noise, I always look up. So many planes. So many people going somewhere. Occasionally a really big plane will fly over. Sometimes it will be from London or going to London. This is exciting to me, to think of a plane full of several hundred people all going to London or having just returned. I wish I was with them.

I wish this every time I hear a plane.

The international airline and iconic brand British Airways celebrated its 100th birthday last year. I'm going to celebrate my 20th anniversary flying the airline soon. It's weird to have a relationship with an airline, but I do. They haven't just flown me there they've been a silent partner in helping Anglotopia to get to where it is today. I've been to Britain 20 times and, until 2018, every time I've flown to Britain I've flown on British Airways (the one time I didn't, I still booked it through them, so still counts, right?). It's as integral a part of my Anglophile experience as enjoying a cup of tea or watching a British TV show.

My first flight was in the halcyon days of summer 2001. Long before the September 11th attacks, long enough ago to remember what it was like to fly before that. It was a completely different experience than it is now. My first trip to London came about because my mother and I really wanted to go there and the trip would be my graduation present from high school (I was an excellent student). What made it affordable was a very convincing brochure that arrived in the mail from British Airways extolling what kind of deal we could get if we booked our whole trip with them.

It didn't take much to convince us.

We were so nerdy about that we loved hearing the British accent of the person on the phone when we booked the trip. We planned it for June 2001, right after school finished for the year. I don't remember how much it cost, but I remember it being exceptionally affordable (I would learn why later… when we checked into our hotel). This was back in the day when the airline still sent you actual plane tickets in the mail. I remember with great excitement opening the envelope with the BA Speedbird logo on it and finding our tickets, printed with my name, telling me I would be going to London. After an adolescence of watching Rick Steves on PBS,

I was finally ready to go on my own European adventure.

British Airways has been flying direct to London from Chicago for more than 60 years. They were one of the first transatlantic airlines to make the journey into America's Heartland. Those first flights, which took place on Boeing Stratocruisers, took almost 16 hours to get to London and required two refueling stops. Now, it's much quicker – depending on the jet stream you can get there in as little as 6 hours with no stops required.

I didn't know any of this on my first flight, though. I didn't know anything about British Airways's heritage. I didn't really know much about anything, to be fair. I was only seventeen years old. I just knew they were British, and they were going to take me to Britain for the first time.

We'd gotten to the airport ridiculously early. So early, the check-in desk wasn't open, and they couldn't yet take our bags. We waited like good patient Anglophiles at the front of the eventual line. This was my first time flying internationally and only my second time on an airplane. So everything about the experience was exciting and new and amazing. Most seasoned travelers would find it mundane. Even after 20 trips, I still find it exciting and amazing.

Our flight was BA296 on June 5th, 2001, the second of British Airways's two daily flights to/from Chicago. It was to depart at 8:15 pm, and we would arrive at 10:00 am London time. As we made our way through Security (quicker than it is now of course), we weaved our way to the gate that BA normally used, M11. And there she was.

A big, beautiful, white Boeing 747-400 gleaming in the late afternoon sun. I remember the paint was so white that it was almost blinding. She was clean. The BA 'Speedbird logo was shining in red, white and blue on the side. I couldn't wrap my head around how big the plane was. How did something so massive take off and essentially float through the air? Clearly, magic was used. The Union Jack on the tail warmed my Anglophile heart.

I watched with great excitement as the ground crews did their work – work they do every day, but work for me that was a novelty. Unloading cargo. Loading cargo. Loading bags. Taking the food onboard (would it be terrible?) and inspecting the engines and fueling up for the flight to London.

Every moment was exciting. Every announcement was exhilarating. In this instance, the journey was just as awe-inspiring as the destination. When our ticket was finally taken, and I was allowed to enter the jet bridge, I practically held my breath in anticipation. If this was living, then I always wanted to be this alive.

I shuffled with the other Economy passengers to the door. I was greeted by a British Airways person, resplendent in their blue uniform, who kindly took my ticket, looked at it and directed me to my seat. And then I set foot on a jumbo jet for the first time. It was noisy. The engines were loud, the air circulation was loud.

But amongst all the noise of the plane getting ready to go, and the people shuffling to their seats, and cabin crew talking, there was the quiet sound of classical music. The Flower Duet by Delibes. The official British Airways theme. I had a feeling of ecstasy, of arriving home for the first time. The 747 was bright, spacious and massive. My seventeen-year-old mind struggled to grasp just how large this aircraft was.

We passed through Business class, which had lie flat beds (an innovation that British Airways actually invented), then through World Traveler Plus (premium economy). And finally, we arrived at Coach (or World Traveler as BA euphemistically applies to it). Our seats were in the very back. It was a strange experience, getting on that plane and walking for what seemed like a mile all the way to the end.

I had a slight problem with it all, though. I was on the tail end of a head cold. When I was struck down with it a few days before the trip, I was in terror that it wouldn't go away before the trip, and it didn't. I was congested, I had a runny nose and a terrible headache. But nothing was going to cancel this trip, certainly not a cold. I bought medicine along with me, but nothing was working that well. The medicine would also ensure that I would not sleep that night.

My mother and I saw our row; I was in the window seat. She was next to me in the middle. Eventually, a kindly man filled out our row. The plane rocked and shook as things were put in the cargo hold and various things I had no concept of were done to this jumbo jet, far from its home in London.

Everything was a novelty. Everything was amazing. We had a little packet that had headphones, socks, eye mask, etc. We had inflight entertainment on the seats in front of us, which in 2001 was still a relatively new thing. The flight attendants were British, and they had the most marvelous accents, many of them different from each other. They handed out British newspapers.

It all went by in a blur. Before I knew it, we were taxiing for take-off. Our British pilot was telling us all about our expected arrival in London. How exciting it all was. And when we made that final turn onto the runway, and the four Rolls-Royce engines spooled up, and we were rocketed down the runway and into the air, I had a moment of clarity that, though I hadn't even arrived in Britain yet, if it was half as amazing as this was I would be in love forever.

I still had that cold to contend with. I tried and tried to sleep that first flight over, but I learned that I cannot sleep on airplanes (unless I'm lying down and, even then, not very well). My nose was running, made worse by the dry air. My legs would get sore. I have a small bladder, and every time I had to get up for the bathroom, I felt bad for the whole row of people who had to get out of my way (knowing this now, I always book an aisle seat).

But British Airways did everything right, something they do almost every day of the year. The flight was smooth. The entertainment worked. The food was edible. It went by in a flash. And when we landed in London, I simply could not believe that we were there. When we parked at a remote stand, I stepped off the stairway and onto the concrete of Heathrow. I was on English soil, finally after dreaming of going to England my whole childhood. I'd arrived. And a British Airways 747 had brought me there.

NERY ✳ WEDDING STATIONERY

W.SCRIPTUM.CO.UK

3

Scriptum

FINE STATIONERY

WWW.SCRIPTUM.CO.UK

PUSH

Scriptum

I have many favorite places in Oxford. It's not hard to have many, it's such a beautiful and historic city with much to see and do. Even whittling down my top 10 things was difficult for an article I wrote in the past. By far, though, one of my favorite places is Scriptum. Located on Turl Street, this tiny little TARDIS of a shop is hard to classify, but I guess you would call it a stationery store.

But it's so much more than that.

It's such a perfect little business, located in the most perfect city if you like learning and scholarship. It's a store filled with the wonders of knowledge and creativity that western culture has produced. The biggest thing they stock is stationery, but not the kind of stationery you get at a local office supply superstore. This is quality stationery, made in small quantities, by craftspeople all over the world.

If you're looking for a blank book or journal or diary, this is the place to find it. They have literally every type you can imagine. Looking for a solid leather book to write in? They have it. Looking for a soft leather journal to carry around? They have it. Looking for something to take notes? They have it. And every single one is a beautiful object. Now, to be fair, you have to pay for this quality.

They have pens and paper and wax seals and everything a 'proper' writer needs to feel, well, proper. They have busts of famous literary and historical figures. When you walk around the store, it's a bit like being in a shop in Harry Potter's Diagon Alley. You can even buy quills if you are so inclined. The upstairs is filled with treasures, many you don't expect to find there – along with a collection of beautiful books.

As I write this the shop is closed due to Covid-19 but this is absolutely one of those places I hope returns as soon as they can. It's a treasure in Oxford and I cannot wait to return myself.

If You Have
Any Questions
Please Ask

Clarendon
Benetian Masks
£25

Old Minster Lovell Hall Ruin

It was our last day in the Cotswolds in Oxfordshire. We'd been staying in a nearby hotel, and everyone we encountered told us to see the ruin. So we went because I love a good ruin and if everyone says it's worth seeing then they might be right. Minster Lovell Hall is signposted on all the nearby roads. When driving down the street towards it, it's not clear where it is. It's a bit hidden. Which only adds to the charm.

We parked at the spot that was a makeshift car park. We geared up with our son in the stroller and walked down the leafy lane. It was a sunny and warm English early summer day in May. The birds cooed in the distance and you could hear the nearby River Windrush. It was a glorious day to be out for a stroll. There was a bit of pressure to see the ruin and move on to our next destination, as I always overpack our research trips with too much to do.

When in doubt follow the signs, and we approached a churchyard. No sign of a ruin. We entered the churchyard and sure enough, behind it, you could see the ruins come into view. We followed the path and there it was, old Minster Lovell Hall, long ago demolished and in pieces. I'm used to seeing old abbey/cathedral or castle ruins all over Britain, but a ruined house is a bit more special as they are rarer.

The house was an important manor hall for centuries in a strategic place along the River Windrush. The Lovell family lost the place after picking the wrong side during the Wars of the Roses. It passed through many hands since then, ending up in the hands of the Coke family. They abandoned the place and moved somewhere else. The house began to be demolished and some of its stones were turned into houses in the surrounding landscape. It has now been ruined longer than it was ever a functioning house.

There is still much left to see including the intricate brick floors and the dovecote, located a short walk away. The whole site is now in the care of English Heritage. Though, as with most places like this, the care is benign neglect. When we visited the garbage bins were overflowing and there were local teenagers sunbathing. Still, it was a lovely atmospheric place, the sounds of the nearby river were relaxing. It was a lovely setting and a lovely ruin, very much worth visiting.

Hardknott Roman Fort

The reward for the most difficult drive I'd ever taken in my life was supposed to be a Roman ruin. Hardknott Roman Fort is in the middle of nowhere. To get there requires a drive over the Eskdale and Hardknott passes, two of the steepest roads in Britain (at one point the gradient is 30%). Of course, you can go the slow way around the Cumbrian coast, but why make it easy when you're rewarded with incredible views of the Cumbrian fells?

You do not do the Hardknott Pass quickly. It's a slow-going route that takes in small villages, busy towns, and countless hikers and bikers enjoying this beautiful Cumbrian landscape. It's not a route you can follow by driving fast. And that's fine. The slowness is a feature, not a bug. By not going fast, you're sure to savor the scenery around you, even while you're concentrating on driving through one of the most beautiful places I've ever been to.

As I crossed over the final crest of the Hardknott Pass, the old Roman fort came into view. Situated on a promontory with a clear view of the Irish Sea, you can see why the Romans chose this spot for their furthest outpost. It's really surprising how much of the ruin is still there. Much of it was pilfered by locals after the Romans left to build the stone walls that snake through the valley. The only thing that lives in this valley are sheep and they are the symphony soundtrack to your visit to this special place.

The site, now owned by English Heritage, has seen better days (I visited in 2018 so it may have improved by now). Many of the notice boards explaining what you were looking at were damaged or faded to the point you couldn't read them. Still, there was plenty to wander around and see. Most of the former walls were about shin or knee height. You have free rein to wander around and climb over whatever you want. This place has no admission charge, how could there be? Can you imagine the commute of someone who had to work an admission desk here every day?

The fort is beautiful. Stark. Abandoned. It's a hard place. It's exactly as the name describes. But more beautiful than the fort are the views from it. To the east is the Hardknott Pass, which snakes down into the valley, and one can't believe you just drove over it. To the west is the blue and emerald Irish Sea, a hard border for Roman influence in these parts of Britain. All around you are sheep and dry-stone walls. It's an English paradise, one of so many in this wonderful country that I love so much.

Shadows of The Great War

It's the least sexy part of traveling, needing to get some cash. We'd just arrived in London with our 2-year old and our 6-month-old (this was in 2013). We were staying in a flat in Earl's Court and decided to walk down to Gloucester Road to find something to eat and an ATM. We were still a bit jet-lagged, so the walk would do us well. Anglotopia Jr was pleased as punch to stretch his little legs.

Serendipitously, we found the local branch of HSBC. Years earlier, in an attempt to feel more international, I'd set up an account with the HSBC subsidiary in America. It made getting wire transfers from the UK and using bank cards while traveling there much easier. And a good travel perk was that, when we actually traveled in the UK, our bank card was treated as a local card – so no ATM fees and the best interbank US/ UK exchange rate.

For those that aren't familiar with it, HSBC is Britain's largest bank – despite the fact that, until 1997, it wasn't technically 'British' in a local sense – it used to be the Hong Kong Shanghai Bancorp but, when Hong Kong was handed back to the Chinese, the bank decided to do a reverse repatriation and move its corporate headquarters to the UK (it's still very international and calls itself the 'world's local bank'). The bank has a long and storied history and has been around for a very long time.

Anyway, I needed the ATM at the branch on Gloucester Road. We walked in, kids in tow and found the ATM and got the cash we needed effortlessly, it's always nice when something so simple works exactly the way it is supposed to. But something struck me about the bank, it was bustling to be sure. Near the window was a small memorial to staff members who had been lost in the Great War (World War I). It was a tiny little unassuming thing, but next to it were several clearly recently placed poppy wreaths. I was very moved at that moment.

It was one thing for the memorial to still be there after almost 100 years, Britain is filled with forgotten monuments everywhere. But it's another thing entirely for the staff at the bank, who probably aren't even connected to the same bank staff from the early 1900s in any way, and have no connection to who is being memorialized, to still take the time to honor the fallen, even in 2013. Even writing about it now, after all this time, makes me a little emotional. This is one of the things I love about Britain so much – the sense of history but also how that sense is wrapped up in never forgetting. World War I was a seminal event in British history that completely upended society (arguably more than WWII did). Every year, across the country, on Armistice Day, people stop to remember, even after relatives who fought in it have been long dead.

They are never forgotten.

Even in a shiny corporate bank branch on Gloucester Road.

Jet Lag, Pizza, and Peep Show

We were exhausted. We'd taken a transatlantic flight, landed at Heathrow, rented a car and driven straight to Shaftesbury, Dorset (a good two-hour drive). Even after bathing and napping in the afternoon, by the evening it was a struggle to stay awake. But we always try to make it to at least 9 pm the first day we arrive in Britain as it helps mitigate jet lag. We had to stay awake.

And we were starving.

So, we did the sensible thing and ordered pizza to be delivered to the cottage where we were staying (it was weird to say to the person on the phone that we were staying on Gold Hill). Shaftesbury is a small town, and the only pizza place open that night was one called Pizza Palace (it's not there anymore).

We were in our jim-jams and ready for a night in. While we waited for the pizza to arrive, the debate began on what we wanted to watch on telly. In the sitting room in Updown Cottage, there's a carefully concealed TV in a cabinet, that gets all the British TV channels. The TV had a menu on the screen you could scroll through. There were many, many options. We didn't want to watch a movie as it was likely to put both of us to sleep. We didn't want to watch the news.

Then we saw something unfamiliar in the guide. It was called Peep Show. It sounded seedy. But the guide said it was a comedy. It was only half an hour long, so it would not demand too much of our attention. The description was vague, something along the lines of 'London roommates Jez and Mark survive in modern London.' We turned it on.

We loved it immediately. It was hilarious. The conceit of the show is that you occasionally get the point of view of each of the characters and hear their internal monologue. It's simultaneously interesting and hilarious. Jez and Mark, the main characters, are very real. And I found myself identifying with Mark quite a bit (both of us are World War II buffs). By the end of the first episode we were laughing in stitches and, well, awake.

Then the pizza arrived, with the ring of the old bell in Updown that's the most beautiful sound. We knew we should have eaten at the dinner table, but pizza deserved to be eaten in front of the TV, but certainly not on the nice sofas in Updown Cottage. So, we got a tray, and both of us sat down on the floor with our drinks and ate pizza as we watched Peep Show. It was on all night and, before we knew it, we'd polished off the pizza and watched more episodes than our bleary jet-lagged eyes could count.

The pizza was... crap pizza. But, you know, the good kind of crap pizza. It suited the TV show we were watching perfectly. It was filling. It was hot. It was cheesy.

After numerous episodes, we finally had to throw in the towel. The comfy bed upstairs in the cottage was calling us. When we returned home after that trip, we binged the entire run of Peep Show (and watched the new episodes as they aired for several more years). It's now our go-to show for when we need a British comedy to pick us up.

And on every subsequent trip to Updown Cottage, the first night we're there, we stick to tradition and order pizza for delivery, sit on the floor and watch Peep Show if it's on (and it usually is).

Fiddleford Manor

It's the little things you come across when you're exploring England that stick with you the most. I came upon Fiddleford Manor House completely by chance one day and I was completely enchanted by it.

It was a special day, sometime between Christmas and New Year's when we were in England for the holiday season back in 2013. I was on an expedition around Dorset and Wiltshire with a local photographer to learn to capture the landscape. It was a wonderful day out, exploring the countryside and taking the time to photograph it properly.

As the end of the day we were exhausted but we still had a little bit of daylight. I noticed in one of my apps that we were close to a restored manor house and I asked to make one final stop. The sun would be setting soon, but we had that final golden late afternoon winter sun that I just love – and makes perfect pictures.

When we parked in the car park, we were the only ones there. We went down a small gravel path that led to the house. There was no admissions desk. It was simply unlocked, and we could have a wander around. There was no one there and there was nothing in the house. It had recently been restored so you could marvel at all the architectural details. There wasn't even anywhere to sit.

But it was filled with the golden glow of the Dorset winter sun through the glass that was hundreds of years old. It was magical inside, despite the emptiness.

We lingered for a bit and soaked in the atmosphere. We took pictures, trying to capture the golden sun as best we could. And then we went on our way, pausing to photograph the Stour River at the bottom of the garden that was at a record flood level.

I haven't been back since, but I still think of this place often. It was a massive manor house, the home of an important person, over generations of English history. Lovingly preserved forever.

I need to go back.

Silly Wizard

The mall is abandoned now. The last stores are either closed or in the process of liquidation. When I drive by, I'm filled with sadness. When you're raised in a society that worships consumerism, it's depressing to see a cathedral to consumerism collapse and became a shadow of its former self. I'm mostly sad because it's where I discovered Silly Wizard.

When I was a teenager I never passed up an opportunity to go to the mall with my parents. By this point, I had my own money (from a thriving dog walking business, I've always been an entrepreneur) and they could set me loose, telling me to meet them at a set time. It was only a small amount of freedom, but it was brilliant because I could do whatever I wanted while I was there.

I always went to the bookstore, but it was at the end of the mall. So my first stop was always the music store. I don't remember what it was called, but they sold everything. I was particularly in love with their classical music section and discovered many wonderful pieces of classical music there. I'd learned early on that classical music was a great hobby to have – the CDs were always very cheap so you could get several instead of just one.

I was browsing the classical section, Goldfinger was playing loudly on the loudspeakers, and I didn't really find anything new or anything I was looking for. My hands wandered to the world music section. This was usually the red-headed stepchild of the music store, where they plopped music they had to stock but knew they wouldn't sell very much.

It's the red case that jumped out at me.

It read simply in golden letters Traditional Music of Scotland.

I studied it. Looked at the track listings. I liked Britain. I wondered if I'd like some of the folk music too. I'm one of those weird people that likes bagpipes. I looked at the track listing, and I didn't recognize any of it. All of the bands meant nothing to me. None of the names sounded familiar. And it appeared that some of the words were in Gaelic. What the CD contained appeared to be a mystery. This wasn't one of those stores that would let you listen to a CD before you bought it. So, I had to make a choice. It cost $5.99. A sizable sum of money in the late 90s to spend on something you had never heard before. What sold me was several songs by a band called 'Silly Wizard.' Well, that just sounded cool!

I put my trust in my love of all things British and purchased the CD and took it home. When I played it for the first time, I was hooked from the first song. I could barely understand most of the words but I loved, loved the sound. Silly Wizard appeared to be some kind of rock folk band. They'd taken traditional Scottish songs and set them to modern style music. As I'm typing this, I realize it can sound kind of lame. But it wasn't lame (Jackie is probably reading this paragraph and harrumphing that it does indeed sound lame, she's not a fan).

I loved the songs so much. The evoked this love of the British landscape and rural life that greatly appealed to teenaged angst Jonathan Thomas. I fell in love with the fantasy of a British idyll (and I'm sure any Scottish people reading this are cringing at me calling anything in Scotland British). I listened to that CD over and over. As the years went on, I quickly found all the Scottish Folk music I could ever want to listen to. I've heard the complete works of Silly Wizard and their lead singer Andy Stewart, including his solo albums.

Silly Wizard was one of those stories that could only happen in 70s Britain. They were a bunch of lads just playing down the pub when they were discovered. And they became international stars on the folk music scene. They toured the world bringing their brand of rock Scottish Folk music to the masses. They had their dramas and, of course, it didn't last, and they eventually broke up like the Beatles. Andy Stewart went on to have a successful career on his own.

He would occasionally tour the USA in areas where Scottish people were known to settle. One time I contemplated driving eight hours to listen to him sing live. By that point I was a confirmed fan, and his music really spoke to me on so many levels. And yes, I realize that being a fan of such a strange and obscure type of music is a bit odd. But then I'll be the first to admit that I'm a bit odd. Sadly, I was a poor college student at the time and couldn't afford to do it.

I will always regret that because the story of Andy Stewart doesn't have a happy ending. He stopped touring not long after that. His personal website stopped being updated, and he stopped making new music. It was almost as if he disappeared into the Scottish Highlands, never to return. I learned later that, despite having the incredible voice that he did, his music career was essentially over — killed by the advent of music piracy (sorry Andy, though I did eventually buy all the music legally) and streaming services. He became a well-known cameraman in the Scottish TV and film industry.

In 2015 his sister went public with the news that he'd had some health problems and a failed spinal surgery led to him being paralyzed from the neck down. Now, unable to sing and unable to work, his sister organized a crowdfunding campaign to raise funds for his ongoing health needs. He died of a stroke a few months later. I was devastated by the news. His music has meant so much to me and played such a critical role in my love for Britain; his death left a void in me. There would be no more new Scottish Folk songs from Andy Stewart.

Now, when I listen to that CD, I no longer have the actual disk, but it will exist forever in my digital music archive, I'm taken back to all my early memories of buying the CD and learning to love music I'd never heard before. It taught me to have varied tastes in music. I've never been a huge fan of 'popular' music, but I like to think I make up for that by liking a variety of different kinds of music. Scottish Folk. Classical Music. Electronic. Techno. Classic Rock. And yes, I even like Coldplay.

Silly Wizard will play on in my music library. And I will continue to enjoy it. You should try it too, you might like it. But like Haggis, it's not everyone's cup of tea.

Mysterious Castlerigg

Castlerigg Stone Circle was my first stop on a busy day of sightseeing in the Lake District. Mostly because it didn't have an open/close time so I could go whenever I liked. I chose to go on my way to Keswick, before everything opened.

The satnav in my car had no problems finding it. This Neolithic stone circle was built approximately 4,000 years ago. Like Stonehenge, we don't really know what it was for but the educated guess is that it was used for pagan religious ceremonies of some kind.

It's situated on a green plateau in Cumbria, surrounded by the fells of the Lake District. When I visited there were sheep grazing around the stones. I was the only person there on a sunny and warm summer morning. The only sound for miles around was sheep.

It was certainly a very picturesque place. It's said this is the most visited of several stone circles in the Lake District, but I was the only one there, so maybe? There's also a legend that it's impossible to count the stones as anyone who attempts will come up with a different number than anyone else. There are definitely many stones.

It's a mysterious and interesting place. What it was for, we can only speculate. But you definitely feel a connection with the past when you visit Castlerigg. Unlike Stonehenge, the stones at Castlerigg are not fenced off and you can wander amongst them and even touch them, which is nice. Castlerigg has a solar alignment and is used in modern day solstice celebrations.

I really quite enjoy touching history like this.

Other than wandering around the stones, there isn't really anything else to see or do here. The real star of this ancient site is the landscape surrounding it and you can understand why ancient peoples felt it was an important place, worthy of a temple of some sort.

The site is now owned and managed by the National Trust. Though, judging by the overflowing garbage cans and faded information post, with torn notices, they don't actively manage it. There is no admission charge, you can wander in whenever you like. I bet it would be really cool to visit the spooky place at night – the stars have to be incredible with clear views of the surrounding horizons. It'd also be a nice place for a picnic.

It's a lovely stop on your way to somewhere else in Cumbria. I highly recommend making the time to stop.

Ginger and John Thomas

I face two enormous points of discrimination if I ever move to the UK. My hair is red, and my name is John Thomas.

In Britain, though, you don't have red hair. You're ginger.

And if you're ginger, it's practically a disability. And it's one of the last things that British people can discriminate against people for and most people will be perfectly OK with it. Jokes at the expense of anyone ginger are commonplace, and one of few things left it's OK to joke about.

As a child who grew up with red hair in America, I was abused constantly. This always baffled me. I still don't understand what someone's hair color has much to do with anything. It's the same way in Britain. If you have red hair – you usually have pale skin, freckles (though I don't have many freckles) and burn easily in the sunlight. When you look up the definition of ginger in the Oxford English Dictionary, the first recorded usage of the word dates back to 1823 and simply states the word is 'derogatory, reflecting negative attitudes towards red-headed people.'

I once worked in a fairly progressive office in downtown Chicago. My co-workers were the young hipster types that proliferated in America's major cities in the late Aughts. It was a nice work environment, a welcoming work environment where there was no discrimination, and you could be comfortable being who you are.

One day, I was in a meeting with a bunch of co-workers talking about an issue a client was having.

A female colleague was going off on a rant about something; I don't remember what as with most meetings in a corporate environment, I didn't really care and didn't need to be there.

"… I don't want this to be a red-headed stepchild."

She stopped.

The whole room stopped. And then everyone looked at me. I was doodling on a notebook and looked up.

The colleague who said it was looking straight at me with a look of horror on her face. The look of horror of a person who has gone out of their way their entire adult life to never say something offensive or judge a person on their appearance.

"I. Am. So. Sorry."

I laughed.

I mumbled "It's OK. I probably would have said the same thing."

One of my best friends in the UK is also ginger, and I heard her own husband call her a mutant for being ginger. While it's true that red-headedness is caused by a mutated gene, I felt this was a bit unfair to her (to be fair they love each other deeply). I wonder if it has something to do with there being a high number of red-headed people in Ireland and Scotland, two peoples who've always faced discriminations as 'others' to the English.

I suppose I should be grateful that neither of my children has red hair. Jackie sometimes chooses to be red-headed on purpose (which has baffled our British friends).

Now it's time for young audiences to turn away.

The emails appear like clockwork in my inbox. At least one a month, sometimes more. The subject line is invariably 'John Thomas' or 'your name.'

"Did you know…"

My name is Jonathan Thomas. I quite like my name. And I never knew there was a problem with it until I started having a lot of contact with British people.

You see, the short version of my name… John Thomas… is British slang for male genitalia.

I did not know this until I started Anglotopia and started meeting a lot of British people. Once I knew this, I immediately began to notice British people withholding laughter or giggles when they met me. This is despite the fact my name is not John Thomas. It's Jonathan Thomas. Jon Thomas is the short version I use but, even then, only Jackie calls me Jon. I've never been a John Thomas.

When I wrote Anglotopia's Dictionary of British English a few years ago, some of the reviews were hilarious because British people couldn't believe that someone named 'John Thomas' wrote a book about British slang. And yes, the word is defined in the book.

Why is this? According to the Oxford English Dictionary, the first recorded use of John Thomas in a genital context came in 1890 in a book. It was cemented in 1928 in Lady Chatterley's Lover, "John Thomas! John Thomas!' and she quickly kissed…" I don't need to go on, do I? So, it appears that John Thomas having this meaning isn't even new. So you're not likely to come across many named John Thomas in Britain because people know what it means and certainly wouldn't choose the name for their kid.

This came up for considerable debate when we had our first child, our son. I'm the first of my name – the first Jonathan William Thomas in our family. I was always a bit jealous of my older brother who was a James Douglas Thomas III. I wanted to start my name line and name our son after me. Jonathan William Thomas Jr. But when we discussed this with our British friends they were horrified by the idea.

One said, "Your goal is to live here one day, right?"

"Yes," I responded.

"Why would you do that to a child?"

They were right. One day we will live in Britain, and that will be with a son who's not named Jonathan William Thomas Jr. We went with William Spencer Thomas. My middle name and my grandfather's name. And the middle name was a compromise, named after Winston Churchill (Spencer was one of his middle names).

I much prefer the original definition of 'John Thomas' in British slang terms – it used to be a servant, flunky or footman. Oh well.

Please remember that John Thomas is not my name. And it's not my fault. Neither is my red hair. Sometimes all I can do is simply say, "Well, my name isn't John Thomas. My name is Jonathan."

Finding Tea at Lulworth Cove and the Secret of English Winters

We'd spent the day on the road and this wasn't even on our itinerary. We happened to be nearby and it was serendipity that we'd got to visit. It turned into one of the nicest experiences we had on the entire trip. I'm talking about Lulworth Cove; a half-moon shaped sheltered bay on the Dorset coast. We'd tried several times to visit over the years but never made it. It was February. Yes, we'd gone to the seaside in February, and we weren't the only ones. The winter is a remarkable time to visit England. England in the winter is the 'real England' because it's not swamped with tourists and you get to enjoy the place without crowds and with the British people themselves.

There's a lovely little café right on Lulworth Cove. We stopped for a bit and had a cream tea and enjoyed the sea view out of the window. It was wonderful. Off in the distance you could see the angry winter ocean breaking on the rocks. Inside the cove it was calm and sedate as the water lapped up against the store. There were a few people about. It wasn't that cold, but it certainly wasn't warm enough to swim. Children played in their wellies in the water and on the rocks. It was the perfect way to spend a cold English February day.

If you talk to British people about the weather, they will always apologize for it. If you asked them about English winters, they would tell you to avoid them at all cost. I've learned over the years that they don't tell you this because the weather can be terrible, and they don't want you to have a bad time. No, they tell you this because they really have the country to themselves in the winter months and they don't want anyone to know how truly wonderful it is. English winters are truly spectacular, and it's a great time to explore England.

Stately homes are at their best in the winter. At least when they're open. Most either close for the winter or are only open at the weekends. But a winter's day out at a place like Kingston Lacey is the best way to spend your time. You practically have the house to yourself. There isn't a long line in the café, and you can usually eat your meal in the warmth of the stables and there's no problem finding a table. We've been there in the summer too, and it's still excellent. But that loveliness quotient is depressed the more people there are. There's no room to sit in the café, and there's barely enough room to get around the house without bumping into someone.

No, it's much better on a day when it's empty, and you can wander from room to room as if you have the place to yourself. It almost feels untoward, having a poke around someone's house by yourself. You feel like an intruder. When we visited Chatsworth for the first time, we were the first ones through the gate when the house opened, and we had all the great rooms to ourselves. It was amazing.

Then there's a stately home like Longleat, which is so much more than a stately home. It has a zoo. A zoo that you drive through. In fact it was the first safari park in Britain and pioneered the whole cars mingling with animals thing. A bleak winter's day, when you've all perhaps gotten a little bit of cabin fever, is the perfect time to drive through a safari park located in the Wiltshire countryside. Your kids will laugh with glee when you go through the monkey enclosure and they start climbing all over the car. Though you might freak out slightly when you realize you didn't get the insurance excess policy as you watch the monkeys disassemble the cars in front of you. You feel rather a bit sorry for the animals, who have to live outside in the English winter. The stately lions certainly don't belong there, but they'll still scare the crap out of you when they rub up against your car.

A cozy old English cottage in the winter in paradise. Except when you've run out of firewood because the fire's constantly been going and you can't get any wood delivered. So, good husband that you are, you're sent out in the gloom and the rain between Christmas and New Year's to find some firewood. Thankfully, your wife called in advance to find anyone nearby who would have firewood. The closest place was 45 minutes away — one way. You didn't mind. You had ClassicFM to keep you company as you drove down single-track lanes through the bleak Dorset landscape.

The journey was made all the more worth it when you returned with enough firewood to last the rest of your stay. That sitting room was warm from that fire and the smell of the burning wood was lovely, so that, whenever you smell burning wood in the future, you are taken back to that room, watching telly with your wife while she sipped a glass of wine and the kids slept upstairs.

London is busy with tourists throughout the year, but winter is when London is left mostly to the Londoners. Londoners have to work, so during the week you practically have the museums and attractions to yourself. There are no lines to get into anything. Anyone who has been stuck in a line to get into one of the free museums in the summer can surely appreciate not waiting in line at all — and then having the cavernous galleries all to yourself. It's just you and the Old Masters of English painting or the great artifacts of the plundered British Empire.

I should probably delete this chapter from the book. I'm giving away my biggest secret to enjoying travel in England. If you all start coming in the winter, then all of these points will be moot. So, let's just keep it between us, OK?

I mumbled "It's OK. I probably would have said the same thing."

Where Have I Seen
This House Before?

The apps told us a stately home was nearby. It was the dead of winter in England. The weather was actually rather pleasant, but it was now well after New Year's. We were in the final week of a five-week-long trip to England to experience an English Christmas (this trip took place in 2013/14). And by this point in the trip we were quite ready to go home. But we still wanted to make the most of our time in England. That and we couldn't stand being in our holiday cottage, which we'd rented from a hostile Basil Fawlty-esque landlady. Despite advertising a cottage geared towards families, she seemed quite put out by the fact we actually showed up with children who had the temerity to make messes and get sick.

So we searched the apps for something to do. We were on the edge of the Cotswolds, the western edge, so there was plenty to do. But we didn't really want to spend forever in the car. The National Trust app told us there was a stately home nearby. It was called Dyrham Park. I knew absolutely nothing about it, but I remembered seeing the gatehouse on our way to this cottage. It was not far. It would surely be a nice day out for the family, at least allow us to get some fresh air and get away from Mrs Basil Fawlty.

When we arrived at the National Trust car park, we were greeted with a sight that is quite rare. It was completely empty. No cars around at all. The visitors' center was shut. Apparently, we'd come on a day when the house was closed (travel tip: double-check the app's opening and closing times…). Undeterred, we decided to have a wander around anyway, there were plenty of public footpaths and we would have them to ourselves.

So, we bundled up and loaded up the strollers and began walking down the drive towards the house, which you can't even see from the car park. We had no idea what to expect.

And then, slowly, it came into view. It was a gloriously sunny winter day and the house glowed in the distance in beautiful honey-colored stone. There was a stream next to the driveway, running fast with water, creating a relaxing atmosphere. As we quietly walked down to the house, I had a feeling in the back of my mind.

A feeling of familiarity. I'd seen this house before.

Had it been in a dream? In a book about stately homes? Where had I seen this house before? It was beautiful, a lovely Baroque-style house sitting in the middle of a gap in two ridges, beyond it a view of sublime green rolling hills, even in the winter. The grounds around the house were flooded, and drains were overflowing. A remnant of the terrible storms that had hit most of Britain that winter (we would learn later that's why the house was closed). As we crossed the cattle grid onto the drive directly in front of the house, there was still no one around. It felt like we were trespassing on someone's private home.

I stood there and admired the beautiful place. It was the epitome of an English stately home. Not too grand but sitting comfortably in its landscape. It was showing its age. While it's well taken care of by the National Trust, you can see the stonework has borne the weathering of time. It looks old. It looks like it has always been there.

But where had I seen it before?

And then it clicked with me.

This was the house from the film The Remains of the Day, one of my favorite British films.

I had managed to visit a place that was very special to me, without realizing it. I was standing in front of Darlington Hall. Perhaps the sunny weather led to my memory confusion. Or perhaps I never really gave much thought to Darlington Hall being a real place. But the house was a real place and it was Dyrham Park and I was standing in front of it. I half expected the butler Mr Stephens to walk out of the front door and enquire why we were trespassing on Lord Darlington's property.

The Ravenglass and Eskdale Railway

I arrived at the railway station having just gone through the Hardknott Pass, Britain's steepest road and one of the most challenging and beautiful drives I'd ever taken in my life. While I generally seek out heritage steam railways, in this case I hadn't. I just needed the loo after the long, slow drive through the Pass.

But then I heard a steam train whistle.

And I was sold.

After I'd visited the facilities, I looked at the train schedule. It was early enough in the day that I still had most of it ahead of me, but it was also lunchtime. Looking at my phone to check the time, I realized I had enough time to eat a spot of lunch in the station café and then catch the next train. The trains ran regularly that day, and I could easily fit in the journey to Ravenglass and back before I needed to move on to my next destination.

So I did what any sensible train nerd would do, I bought a ticket, ate my lunch and waited for the next train. The café lunch was your typical heritage railway café fare (an always reliably filling and tasty lunch I have found). I had a burger and chips. It was a very hot day, so I was grateful for the cool place in which to eat lunch.

Now, the Ravenglass & Eskdale Steam Railway isn't a proper 'big' railway. It's a narrow- gauge line, operating with a 15-inch track gauge. The trains are small, I would describe them as cute. The steam engines are in miniature – but they're still proper steam engines. The carriages are small as well, and there's only really room in each carriage for yourself and another adult (or a couple of kids). I was there alone, and I will admit that it did feel a bit odd to be a mid-30s male by myself amongst all the families and retirees. But I would not let something like that get in the way of me enjoying a steam train.

The line runs for seven miles through the beautiful Esk Valley from Dalegarth to Ravenglass (or the reverse, depending on how you want to look at it). The name Ravenglass sounded like a really cool place to visit. It evoked a place from one of my favorite shows, Game of Thrones. The line was originally built in 1875 to service the mines in Cumbria – it carried iron ore from the mines in the Eskdale Valley to the mainline railway in Ravenglass. When mining ended in the mid-20th century, the line was sold off and bought by a preservation society which sought to preserve the line, protect its heritage, and open it up to tourists.

It is now one of the most popular tourist attractions in the Lake District. The main attraction of the line, other than a day out on a miniature steam train, is the landscape around it. The seven miles of rails go through the Eskdale Valley, west to the sea. You can enjoy views of the Cumbrian fells, including Scafell Pike, the tallest.

I took a seat on the train, picking a covered carriage but one that was still open to the elements. It was very hot that day, and I figured once the train got moving it would be the most comfortable. The open top carriages did not appeal to this pale ginger bloke who would roast in the open sun. And closing myself off in one of the enclosed, ancient carriages, seemed like a recipe for heat stroke. It must have seemed an odd scene to the other passengers. A middle-aged American man, in shorts and a baseball cap, striding the single car just big enough to contain him as the small steam train chuffed through the Eskdale Valley.

The train got underway right on time, there was ample steam tooting, which delighted the twelve-year-old in me. The train moved at a gingerly pace. The goal of journeys like this isn't to get to the destination as quickly as possible but to enjoy the journey itself. It was hot, but not too uncomfortable once the train got moving. It was a weekday, so the train was not too full.

The landscape of the Eskdale Valley is breathtakingly beautiful. And it was a pure joy to be there on a warm day, soaking in the full greenness of the valley in its summer glory. The train ride was 40 minutes – 40 minutes to go just seven miles. Which was fine, despite having a lot to cram into the day, I was in no real hurry. The summer days in Northern England are long, I had plenty of daylight ahead of me.

Along the way, there were several stops, called Halts. Some it stopped at. Some it just steamed on by. We occasionally had to stop to let another train pass (and got to watch them pass the signal baton – which was neat).

Soon we arrived in Ravenglass, which is actually a mainline railway station, where you can catch the trains that go up and down the Cumbrian coast. Until that day, I had never heard of Ravenglass and had no idea what there was to see there. So I quickly walked out of the station and into the village. Not knowing where to go, I just followed all the elderly passengers walking into the town. I could smell the sea.

As I walked onto the main street of the village and then over to the views of the estuary, where the tide was out, I looked around hopefully. There really wasn't anything to see or do. Since the tide was out there were no beautiful views of the estuary other than a few boats in the mud. There was a pub, but I'd just eaten, and I don't drink, so a warm pint on a hot day didn't appeal. I had no phone signal so I couldn't see what was

around. So I did what any sensible travel writer does in a hurry; I turned around and walked right back to the railway station.

There was a museum there about the history of the railway, but I decided to give it a pass so that I could catch the next train, if I missed it I would have to wait an hour for the next one and, as there was nothing to do in Ravenglass, I did not want to spend any more time there (Muncaster Castle, which was nearby, was beckoning).

The steam train ride back to Dalegarth was a bit less enjoyable than the ride to Ravenglass. It'd gotten hotter. The novelty of the train ride to Ravenglass made the journey enjoyable. The 40-minute ride back, the novelty had worn off, and I was quite ready to be done with the miniature steam train for the day. But I tried to sit back and take in the scenery, it really was beautiful. Everywhere in Cumbria is beautiful. Up until that point, it'd had been the most beautiful place I'd ever been.

The train finally arrived back in Dalegarth, and your hot and sweaty writer hopped back into his cool, air-conditioned car and went on to his next destination: Muncaster Castle. I said goodbye to the Eskdale Valley. Would I visit the railway again? Not by myself, but I'd come back with my kids, they would love it (and they loved the souvenirs I picked up for them in the gift shop). I think I might quite like to do the walk that follows the railway line – to take the train one way then walk back. Overall It was a lovely, sedate day on the Ravenglass & Eskdale Railway. Steam trains, pretty landscapes, the sea, families having days out, tea and cake, a beautiful English summer day – what's not to love?

High Altar

The Tree in the Ruin
and £50 Notes

When I'm traveling I often get an early start as I'm always so excited to get going and explore that I hit the road as soon as I've eaten breakfast. Often times, though, the problem with this is that I get too early of a start. Being on the road by 9 am is good and all if you have a long drive. But I've found that, most of the time, tourist attractions in Britain don't open until 10 am or 11 am. So I usually find myself sitting in a car park, reading my phone, while I wait for something to open.

I'm always attracted to a good ruin. This one wasn't on my itinerary, but I needed something to do until a larger tourist attraction opened, and Bayham Abbey was on the way. Of course, I arrived too early. So early, that the gates to the road weren't yet open. So I drove around the area to see what was nearby. When I returned, the gate was open. But the attraction hadn't opened. So, I got out of the car and walked around the car park and wandered over to the view of New Bayham Abbey, a privately-owned stately home that wasn't open to the public. Even that didn't kill enough time.

When the gates finally opened, I entered the tiny little shop and was presented with a very flustered Frenchwoman working the till, who was still doing all the things she needed to do to open the place. When I went to pay for my ticket, I handed her a £50 note. She balked.

Now, this was all I had on hand. In Britain, though, a £50 note is equivalent to a $100 bill (there isn't a £100 note in England). Most places don't like to take them and, if they do, they might not have enough change to break one. So this poor girl, clearly flustered by the large bill, immediately had a meltdown. Muttering in French and English, "I have to open zee safe to break this, my non." Or something like that.

Eventually, she made the change and I made haste to explore the ruin. It was much calmer in the ruin than it was in the tiny ticket office. The abbey ruin was mostly unremarkable by ruins' standards. Except for a tiny little thing that most people probably wouldn't even notice. Located by the former high altar was a tree, hundreds of years old, whose roots had become part of the wall. It was difficult to tell what was holding up what at this point. The wall had become the tree and the tree had become the wall. It was quietly beautiful. I stood there in the drizzle and admired it for quite some time. Henry VIII struck this place down and stole its wealth. But life still found a way to endure in this quiet spot in southeast England. It had very much been worth the stop.

Hardy's Birthplace

My love for Dorset goes hand in hand with my love of the literary works of Thomas Hardy, a man more associated with Dorset than any other. So it's been a goal for me for a long time to visit his birthplace, deep in the Dorset countryside. Not just because of its connection to the man but also because it has a beautiful setting and I thought a picture of it would go nicely in the Anglotopia Calendar.

I'd been to Dorset more times than I could remember and still hadn't managed to visit his birthplace. It was either closed for the season or didn't fit into an itinerary. On a recent trip, after visiting nearby Kingston Lacey, we had a couple of hours left on a beautiful afternoon and decided to make a run for it. We had no kids with us and hopefully plenty of time to see it.

I was also quite keen to visit because I'd heard there was a modern visitors' center nearby that was just finished. I wanted to take a look and see if it was as nice as it was planned to be.

We made it just in time.

The National Trust owns and runs the cottage as part of its network of properties. We visited using our Royal Oak passes, so admission was free. The cottage was built by the Hardy family, and it's where Thomas was born. It's made of local building materials and is very much in the vernacular of the area. Hardy grew up in the house and its rural setting amongst farm fields, woodlands and villages was his inspiration for the settings of his stories. You can certainly get the same feeling – Bockhampton is still a small village, and it's very quiet. The house is surrounded by gardens and woodlands, so it's a very peaceful and inspirational place.

We arrived at about 4 pm; the last admission was at 4:15, so we had to be quick about it. We parked in the new county-owned free car park, which is located by the new visitors' center. The problem, though, was that the center was closing when we arrived. By the time we returned from the cottage, it was shut completely, so we weren't able to explore the gift shop to treat ourselves to any National Trust cakes. It seems a bit odd for the visitors' center to close an hour before the actual attraction.

We followed the signs to the cottage, and this is where it got a bit annoying really. The cottage is very far from the visitors' center. You have to go on a walk through the woods along a well-manicured path. The path is very nice, but it's long, and it varies in terrain. After spending most of the day on our feet already, we were not expecting a walk. We

71

were also very conscious of how much time we had, and we had only just made it to the gatehouse before the last entry.

However, you can see that the intention behind the walk is to create a sense of place, and it works. The cottage is sitting perfectly in its environment and, when you round the corner and see it, nestled in the woods and its lovely gardens, it clicks with you why they chose this method of arrival. The problem is that the elderly or disabled may have issues going down the path – so there is a different way to approach that's flat and follows the main road in Bockhampton (follow the signs).

The house is quite small and, in fact, at one time it was two houses – Granny had her own house. When she passed on, the house was knocked together, and at one point there were seven people living in it. The cottage is typical of a Dorset cottage; it's small, has low ceilings and tiny bedrooms. It's a very intimate home as a modern real estate agent would probably describe it. This is how life was lived during the Victorian Age, so there are many Victorian-era flourishes.

We pretty much had the place to ourselves. Inside the house, there was a room guide who filled us in on a lot of the history we wanted to know, and then we were left to our own devices to explore the house.

Far from the Madding Crowd is one of my favorite books, so it was a treat to see the room and the very desk where he wrote it (apparently, the actual desk is in the Dorset County Museum, this is a replica). It didn't take long to have a poke around the cottage, take some pictures and be on our way.

I must say that the gardens are beautiful. It was early May when we visited, so things were just coming into bloom. The garden is laid out much as it was when the Hardy family left the cottage and rented it out. I'm glad to see the National Trust keeping up the gardening traditions started back then.

A little bit of trivia, there is actually a private apartment nestled on the second floor of the house where one of the property managers lives. I read on the BBC a while ago that there's actually an American academic living there. How does one get that job? I should also note that Thomas Hardy did not spend his whole life here. He grew up there, spent time away in London, came back and eventually built himself a new house in Dorchester at Max Gate once he became a famous author. But he and the family still maintained their connection to the place until well into the 20th century.

We walked back through Bockhampton, a very lovely walk. It was the late afternoon, it was quiet, and the flowers were beautiful – not to mention the lovely Dorset cottages that lined the road. You can see what the Hardy family saw in the place, and I'm very happy to see that it still maintains its rural character – as Hardy would have wanted.

Eggs and Toast on Gold Hill

I'm a big believer in eating breakfast (Mrs Anglotopia is not). I'm the kind of person that can't function without a good breakfast. When I travel to Britain, one thing I look forward to most is breakfast. Now this isn't going to be an essay about how glorious the 'Full English' is, and it is. It's about my preferred breakfast, which is infinitely times more satisfying in Britain than it is back home. Scrambled eggs and toast, sometimes with British bacon too.

It's the simplest of breakfasts. Scramble some eggs, fry some bacon, make some toast, wash it down with orange juice and tea. I treat myself to it at least once a week. I follow Gordon Ramsey's scrambled eggs recipe (eggs, milk, butter, stir in the pan until they're done to your taste – only add salt and pepper afterwards). When we stay in self-catering accommodation one of the things I look forward to most is making my own breakfast and, as a creature of habit, I eat the same thing pretty much every day.

I love going into a British grocery store and buying the ingredients for my British breakfast. I buy British milk. I buy British eggs (which, oddly, sit on a shelf and not in the fridge section). I buy British butter. I buy some British bacon. And the most critical items of all: bread for toasting and orange marmalade. Then it's back to the cottage to cook on the stove. It's a quick breakfast to make. The hardest part is timing the bacon and toast to be done at the same time as the eggs. I like all my food done at the same time and equally hot. And don't forget to put the kettle on for tea afterwards.

I've tried to replicate this breakfast back home, but it never tastes as good as it does in Britain (so I make it a little differently at home). It must be the quality of the ingredients, the richness of the eggs and milk and butter. British bread is the best bread. Then when you butter the bread with British butter and then slather marmalade on top.... Mmm, I'm salivating as I write this. British eggs taste richer than at home and when you scramble them they're airy and delicious. It's the perfect fuel for a day of exploring England. Even when we stay in hotels, I'll usually have this same breakfast, mostly because it's the easiest thing for poorly made hotel breakfasts to get right.

But then the location is also key. When I make breakfast in my favorite place, Updown Cottage in Shaftesbury, Dorset, I make the food on the best cookware and stove possible. Then it's to the dining room next to the kitchen, which has the most incredible view of the Blackmore

Vale. Eating a perfect breakfast, made with British ingredients, washed down with orange juice (with bits, as the carton says) and tea is the perfect way to start the day. The morning sun through the windows is simply heaven; Anglophile Nirvana. The food is heaven. Music playing on the radio is heaven. The simplest food can be the best meal you've ever had when it's in the perfect place.

Muncaster Castle

Muncaster Castle was my third destination on my final day exploring the Lake District. By the time I arrived at Muncaster Castle I was, to say the least, exhausted. But it was my final day of traveling and seeing a castle was the perfect way to end my trip.

I visited this castle knowing absolutely nothing about it, having only heard about it during my time in the Lake District when I was looking for something to do.

Muncaster Castle is situated on the very western edge of the Lake District. It's in a very strategic place, up a rise that has an all-around view of the Esk Valley and the sea beyond. There is evidence of Roman settlement; even the Romans thought this was an important spot – Hardknott Roman Fort is just a few miles away.

The castle is owned by the Pennington family. In fact, it has always been owned by the Pennington family. They have recorded evidence of this historic house being their home since 1208 when lands around it were granted to Alan de Penitone. As with all things that old, the date is flexible. There are some records that go back even further suggesting that the family have been here since at least 1026.

The current generation of the family runs the property as a charity and opens it to visitors. Unlike a National Trust or English Heritage property, it's very much a private home still; the website says they live in the servant's quarters nowadays. It definitely feels a lot more authentic and lived in than one of Britain's 'GREAT' stately homes. I quite like this.

The castle was built in the late 13th century and enlarged in the 14th. Like all old castles like this, it has been added on and modified for its entire history. Its current form was finalized in the Victorian era by the fifth Baronet of Muncaster. It started to resemble more of a stately home than a proper castle (most of Britain's 'castles' ended up as faux castles or stately homes eventually – that or ruins).

I parked in the car park, which was across the street from the entrance. It was a weekday in July, and I was surprised to be one of the few cars in the car park. I crossed the busy street (actually the main road through this part of the Lake District) and made my way to the ticket office. A modern construction, there was a kindly older lady selling tickets and helpfully handing out maps.

My heart dropped a little bit when she told me that the castle was actually half a mile from where I was standing. I'd had a very long day

already, and my feet were not happy about this. But still, castles are always worth it, aren't they? Besides, walks will not kill me. In fact, walking often will keep me alive longer. So, I soldiered on.

I walked my way on a nicely finished path, through woodland with ancient trees. It was somewhat magical and, despite the heat, I was quite enjoying my late afternoon stroll to a castle.

I came around a bend and there it was, Muncaster Castle. It was indeed impressive, and I have seen a lot of castles in my day. The architectural style is a mixture of medieval castle and Victorian faux-castle architecture. It gels together quite well. Built in the warm reddish stone of the nearby hills, it creates a pleasing look to the eye. I hadn't even been inside, and I already quite liked the place.

I followed the path along the side and then around to the front where the visitors' entrance was. Only I didn't go in immediately. There were a series of benches on the front, and you could clearly see why they were there – the view back up the Esk Valley was simply incredible. Perched on its promontory, you can see why they built a castle here. Perfect for defense and keeping an eye on things, now it was perfect for creating beautiful views. I felt very lucky to be standing there.

You could see the Esk River, winding its way through the valley, along with the roads snaking their way through challenging geography. Off in the distance were the western Cumbrian fells, including Scafell Pike, the tallest mountain in England. It was a gloriously clear day with beautiful blue skies. The world was mostly silent, and you could clearly hear your own thoughts. There really isn't much more perfect than this.

I walked around the castle and took plenty of pictures. Always good to have as many pictures of Britain's famous castles as possible, you never know when you're going to need them (and not just for this book). When I finally went in, I was warmly greeted by the attendant.

"Hello," she said, "I saw you taking pictures outside! What a lovely camera."

It was at that point I learned the one thing I dread most of all visiting Britain's stately homes; in this one, I would not be allowed to take pictures. They were very friendly about it, and I had to turn over my backpack and camera while I had a wander around. The attendant was very helpful in directing me in where to go.

The rooms are set out on a self-guided tour path. I took the option of listening to the recorded tour on a handset. It was pretty easy to follow, you simply enter the number of whatever room you are in. There were usually two narrations, the official history of the room and its contents, and then another by a member of the family giving a more personal context. It was all very interesting. Sadly, I don't really remember much

from it as I couldn't take notes and it was almost a year ago now. I am currently admonishing Past-Jonathan for not taking better notes when he left the castle.

Each room was marvelously appointed with centuries of family artifacts, kept in a tasteful manner so as not to be overwhelming. The place had the most remarkable smell; I love the way these old places smell.

My favorite room was the library. When I entered the castle's beautiful octagonal Victorian era library, I was in complete awe and then suddenly shocked to see a person sitting at a stately desk pouring over some ancient text.

Had I just stumbled upon the Lord of the Manor studying in his library? I suddenly felt like I was invading this quiet, cloistered place. I was the only other person in there, and I felt like I was intruding on the Lord of the Manor studying in his library.

But I'd paid to get in! Surely, he wouldn't mind.

So, I wandered around the room and admired all the books. It was really a dream library. An incredible space. One of the most beautiful libraries I have ever seen. That's not even mentioning the view from the massive single pane windows across the valley out of one side and the sea on the other side.

As I got closer to the big desk, I was relieved to see that there was a volunteer badge on the gentleman at the desk, and I suddenly felt at ease admiring this space. I wasn't intruding.

My tour of the rooms did not take much longer and, before I knew it, I was back outside. I wandered around the grounds, walking the footpaths around the castle. Muncaster is famous for its Hawk & Owl Centre, which cares for the special birds. They have regular falconry shows, but I was there at a time when there wasn't one on (though I did see a chap practicing with a falcon off in the distance). The aviary was very cool, they had many impressive birds on display though most of them were having an afternoon nap during my visit and the cries of a young baby owl, seemingly searching for its lost mother, were rather distressing. The center does important conservation work for owls and hawks. I really like seeing places like this and giving the public access like this is wonderful. I shall have to return when there is a show on. I'd recently read H is for Hawk by Helen Macdonald – one of the finest books I've ever read – so it was interesting to see real hawks in the flesh, as I don't see many around here in rural Indiana where I live.

One thing I loved about Muncaster was its absolutely remoteness. It's very far away from everything. Driving here to this far end of the Lake District from anywhere will take several hours; it took me two hours to get back to my hotel later! A train ride will take several hours. You can't fly here. Even if you're already in the Lake District, it takes some effort to get here. I loved its romantic isolation. It was quiet. The only occasional sound was a car passing through the Esk Valley. I was suddenly very envious of the family that gets to call this special place home.

There was more to see and do at Muncaster – including a church on the grounds and miles of footpaths. But my feet had had enough, and they were already screaming about the walk back to the car park. So,I bid farewell and headed back to my car. I quite liked Muncaster Castle and would very much like to go back. I think staying at the B&B on site would be peaceful and lovely.

I drove back to my hotel near Penrith, enjoying the late afternoon golden sunshine as I traveled along the coast and peninsulas of the southwestern Lake District. It was the perfect way to end my visit to the Lake District. I can't wait to go back.

The Best Café in Oxford

I've spent a lot of time in Oxford. It's my favorite city in Britain outside of London (in fact, I might like it more than London - shhhh!). From day trips to long stays in the summer for a course, I've spent a lot of time there. I have my own haunts that I enjoy very much. Of course, I like places like the Eagle and Child and Blackwells. But my favorite place to eat is Brown's Café in the Oxford Covered Market (not to be confused with the Browns restaurant chain).

This lovely little place has been there since 1924, almost a hundred years in the same family and a mainstay of Oxford locals and students for as long as it has been there. Stepping into the place is like stepping back in time. It's a traditional old British café. You can get a cup of tea or coffee or you can get a meal. And the variety of meals available is mind-boggling. The place is so small, you wonder where they store all this food!

The food is hearty British fare, but there's also a flare for various other types of dishes from all over the world. I much prefer the British fare. You can get reliably tasty meat pies, bangers & mash, roasts, chicken – even burgers (definitely not British). The chunky chips on offer are delicious, especially when soaked in their house gravy. You order at the counter, and they bring the food to you when it's ready. Best of all, the food is very reasonably priced. You can easily eat a freshly cooked meal for under a tenner.

Eating here is like being a temporary local, which is the best way to travel. It's a quiet little oasis in busy Oxford. People walk by, students eat their lunches, people read newspapers, study books, play on their phones. The lighting is warm; the place is especially inviting on a cold winter's day, serving hot tea and warm food. When I've needed a quick and yummy meal while in Oxford, this place has saved me more than once. It's a treasure.

It's had a starring role in Oxford's famous TV shows – Morse, Lewis and Endeavour. It's fun to spot it in the show, knowing I've been there. There's been talk of changes at Oxford Covered Market – rising rents are pushing out mainstay businesses – one hopes Brown's Café is able to endure. It's a treasure of a place serving delicious food. Try to have lunch there when you're in town. It's well worth it.

Kipling's Rest

When I visited the home of Rudyard Kipling, Bateman's, it was serendipitous. I'd had a busy day exploring Kent, and my itinerary took less time than I'd allocated, mostly because it was raining on and off during the day so I couldn't spend a lot of time outside. So, with some extra free time, I decided to direct the car SatNav to Bateman's when I discovered it was nearby.

Kipling is out of fashion. Granted his classic stories like The Jungle Book continue to endure and have been adapted into several successful films, but that's because that story has become part of the cultural zeitgeist and can easily be scrubbed of its Imperialism. But if there is one British writer who is associated with the spirit of the former British Empire, it is Kipling. And that makes him problematic in our more enlightened times.

I find Kipling to be a tragic figure. Sure, he was a big proponent of the Empire he served with the pen, but his own son died directly as a result, he even pulled strings to get his son enlisted. On a personal level, I admire his catalog of works, his stature as a man of letters, so I was very excited to visit his home.

Kipling had this to say about the house in 1902: "We have loved it ever since our first sight of it… We entered and felt her spirit – her Feng Shui – to be good. We went through every room and found no shadows of ancient regrets, stifled miseries, nor any menace, though her new end was three hundred years old… a real house in which to settle down."

He probably wouldn't have said the same thing about the house after living in it for almost 40 years. If you didn't know the house had any connection to Kipling, you would probably agree with him. It is a very agreeable looking old English house. It is not grand like Blenheim or Chatsworth. It's very much the humble home of a writer as you would expect. It's a true English idyll, surrounded by beautiful gardens and grounds which, due to rain, I didn't have a chance to explore that day.

The house was built in 1634. For historical perspective, this was the reign of Charles I (when he was in his dictatorial phase that led to his eventual trial and beheading). The Plymouth Massachusetts colony was still new and struggling. The Reformation was still burning across Europe. It was a turbulent time, but that is not reflected in the Jacobean style of architecture used for this house.

There is debate as to the original builder. Historic England follows the tradition favored by Kipling of ascribing the construction to a Sussex ironmaster, a certain John Britten. The historian Adam Nicolson reports

the tradition in the National Trust's guidebook but notes that Britten was a dealer in iron, rather than a manufacturer. The architectural historian Nicholas Pevsner attributes the construction to a lawyer, William Langham. It doesn't really matter, the house exists, and it's beautiful.

The house is built of sandstone to a double-pile plan and has two stories with gables above. The eastern entrance front may once have been symmetrical with a northern wing matching the southern one. Historic England's listing states that the wing was constructed but later torn down, while Pevsner suggests that it may never have been built. The windows are mullioned, and the roof has an "impressive row of six diamond-shaped red brick chimney stacks."

The interior of the house is retained as it was in the time of the Kiplings. The study is almost as Kipling left it, although without the "pungent aroma" of his forty-a-day Turkish cigarette habit. The house contains a significant collection relating to Kipling, amounting to nearly 5,000 individual pieces, including his Nobel Prize, his Rolls-Royce Silver Ghost (in the garage of course), many Oriental items he purchased while living in India or touring in the East and paintings he collected by Edward Poynter, Edward Burne-Jones, and James Whistler. The garden was created by Kipling in 1907, using the prize money from the Nobel Prize in Literature.

By the early twentieth century, the house had descended to the status of a farmhouse and was in a poor state of repair. The Kiplings first saw it in 1900, on returning to England from America, following the death of their daughter Josephine in 1899 (she inspired his Just So stories and then tragically died). Enchanted by the house, they were too slow in making an offer, and it was let for two years instead. In 1902 they were able to purchase it with 33 acres of land. When the Kiplings purchased the house, Rudyard was one of the most famous living writers in the world so could afford such a house. He lived there until he died in 1936. His wife continued to live there until her death at which point it was left to the National Trust for preservation.

When I arrived I discovered the house was a short walk from the car park. It was raining a bit, so I took my trusty travel umbrella with me. When I entered the house, the staff provided a plastic wrapping for my umbrella so that its wetness didn't damage any contents in the house. Leave it to the British to have all eventualities in place for rain. The house was not too crowded though I did get the sense that perhaps quite a few people visiting the property were trying to stay out of the rain.

My favorite room was the study, which was left much as it was when he was working there. It's exactly the kind of space you'd imagine an early 20th-century British writer to have. Books upon books, papers upon papers, Imperial artifacts cluttering every surface. A most wonderful old house smell. I took particular joy in spotting the little stuffed mice around the house that have been left out for children to find while they go through the house, lest they get bored.

If you're in the area of East Sussex and are interested in British Imperial history and literature, then I highly recommend a visit to Bateman's.

Midnight in the Lake District

In the summer in the Lake District the sun simply does not set. Well, it does technically. It goes over the horizon. You just can't actually see it anymore. But it never gets completely dark. The sky stays a dark crimson blue, even past midnight. It's a magic hour until well after midnight and it's very alluring and otherworldly at the same time. Most of the stars don't even come out, and the ones that do, really want you to see them.

When I visited the Lake District in July 2018 for a writing retreat, our speaker dinners would often go late into the night and a vigorous group of creative people would talk about writing and the craft, discussing ideas from the brains of some of Britain's best writers. On leaving these dinners at almost midnight, I would drive along Ullswater from Glenridding and the entire landscape, which only the day before was shining brilliantly green in the golden English summer, was a muted blue. Misty and blue and dark. The mountains around Ullswater were like ghosts, slightly there but slightly not. It was otherworldly.

It was just dark enough to make driving dangerous. I'd done the drive countless times that week, so I never felt like I was in danger. But I had to pay extra attention, even while I was in awe of the landscape around me. It's strange trying to sleep in this land that never gets dark. I found myself having to draw the curtains in my hotel room shut every night, it just wasn't dark enough outside for me. I'd still keep the window cracked though, to let in the cool night breeze and to hear the bleating of the Hardwick sheep around the hotel.

There weren't many stars out, which disappointed me slightly. I'd heard the Lake District was as Dark Sky Reserve and I'd actually brought stuff with me to stargaze at night, including a special red flashlight. But, alas, I never needed any of it. There weren't many stars to see, it just didn't get dark enough. The dark skies only apply when it's not summer. Really, the only two stars in the sky were not stars, they were planets. Jupiter and Venus on opposite ends of the horizon for part of the night. When I returned one night from Keswick, I stood outside and admired both, thinking of the orbital ballet that led to their positions so perfectly just above the mountains of the Lake District horizon.

One night, I was so tired, I'd forgotten to shut my curtains. And when I got up to use the loo in the middle of the night, my room was still filled with the strange blue half-light. I paused and soaked it in. The silence of the landscape around me filled the room. It was one of life's perfect moments. Everything was at peace. The dark blue night sky. The sheep outside. The gentle breeze across the landscape. When you visit the Lake District in the summer, you don't want the days to end, and they really don't. It's heaven.

Getting Lost in the
Search for Melbury Hill

We were trudging along a path through a field. It was beautiful. It was a gloriously sunny day in spring, perfect for a walk in rural Dorset. Our goal for the day was to walk to Melbury Hill and for most of the time we could see ourselves walking towards it. But now we could no longer see the hill, and I wasn't entirely sure we were in the right place. With my handy Ordnance Survey Map in hand (number 118), I paused to figure out just where we were. My fiancée, Jackie, was getting increasingly annoyed with me and I had the sinking feeling that we were hopelessly lost.

Our journey had started the year before in the Travel Bookshop in picturesque Notting Hill in London, made famous by the film of the same name. The bookshop is no longer there, but in the early 2000s it was a must-stop for fans of the eponymous film. When I visited for the first time, I also discovered something I'd never seen before: Ordnance Survey maps.

We have no equivalent here in the United States. If I wanted a helpful map that perfectly laid out the geography around my house, along with public rights of way and interesting things to see along the way, I would be disappointed. It simply doesn't exist. When I first cracked open map 118 in that bookstore in London, I was entranced. Here was a detailed map of my favorite place, Shaftesbury, Dorset, and the surrounding lands. It was like finding a map of Middle-Earth: I had found a map of my secret place, and it would tell me where everything was.

I happily paid £6.99 for that map, which was a lot in my poor college student days.

For the next year, I got lost in that map. It became a personal totem. I would carry it with me everywhere; these were my university days, so I always had my backpack with me. Whenever I had a break between lectures or time in the library to research the latest boring paper I had to write, I would pull out that map and study it. Its language was foreign to me, and I was determined to learn it. I wanted to return to Dorset and let it guide me amongst the hills around Shaftesbury. By doing this, I would no longer just love Gold Hill, but I would tread everywhere within the famous view and know the place much more than a simple tourist snap allows.

When it came time to return to Shaftesbury, I'd made great preparations to go on my first walk with my OS Map. I'd done my

homework and planned my route meticulously. I'd even done something horrible: I'd taken a highlighter and drawn our complete route (I would never do this now! I was young and naive, please forgive me). We were going to follow the roads and public footpaths from Shaftesbury and walk to Melbury Hill and climb it.

Melbury Hill is the large hill you always see in the background of pictures of Gold Hill. To prepare for the walk, I'd even bought my first pair of rubber Wellington boots (from before they were sold off and began to be manufactured in China – my wellies are PROPER), and I had a waterproof coat, so was prepared for any weather. When I told our innkeeper at the B&B we were staying at on our route, he was impressed and wished us well.

So, we departed early. We followed my route meticulously. When we ran into a local rather worryingly carrying a chainsaw, he said "Good Morning."

"Good morning," I replied.

"Americans, eh?" Even two words give away our accent and the fact we are not locals and never will be.

We nodded.

"Lovely day for a walk, just on my way to trim a hedge for a friend," he said noticing my orange OS map. "Where you headed?"

"Melbury Hill."

"You're on the right road, French Mill Lane. Just keep following it to the end and then turn left."

It gave me far too much confidence that I knew what I was doing. We continued following French Mill Lane and then came to our first public footpath, which I was very excited to traverse. It was so strange to be on a public footpath. It was like we'd entered a secret world. The road disappeared, and we were on someone's land, but the path was a clear way through and, according to the map, we had every right to do so. Coming from the land of the 'no trespassing' sign, this was all quite disconcerting.

So I shouldn't be surprised at what happened next.

I guess I didn't study the map well enough. I began to curse myself for being a bad Boy Scout. I never did earn my Orienteering badge. I could hear my Scoutmaster laughing at me in the back of my head (I was, generally, a terrible Boy Scout – I still can't start a fire properly).

I simply could not find us on the map. The pressure and stress of not being able to perform made me sweat. All the lines on the map began to blur together. The map key escaped my head completely, and I couldn't remember what anything meant. We came across a busy road and began following that, but that was not the route I'd planned for months. Cars zoomed by until we came across another footpath. I'll never forget the look of fear combined with consternation on Jackie's face.

We walked further, past quaint cottages and more fields. I still could not figure out where we were. We followed another road.

At this point, Jackie was getting quite cross at the man she was with who couldn't read the map he'd been obsessing over for a year. Neither of us was going to admit out loud that we were lost. The reality of mistranslating the lines on a map versus the real world was just too much for my inexperience. Miraculously, she didn't take the map out of my hands and take over. We continued on, lost, but we could see Melbury Hill so figured we were going in the right direction.

But while we were lost, we were lost in a beautiful landscape. My digital camera, back then they were still a relatively new technology, got quite a workout as I took picture upon picture. At one point, we walked through someone's farm, and that was so strange. We peeked into his empty barn. Artsy photos were taken. But we could not shake the feeling that we were trespassing even though we weren't. This was freedom, the right to roam!

Eventually, I found us on the map again, and we found our way to Melbury Abbas, the small village at the base of the hill (which oddly has an American style mailbox at one of the houses). The hill had been this distant thing our whole walk, and for my whole year previously, and here we were, right in front of it. It was rather surreal.

And we were absolutely shattered. Having not been on many long walks for the previous year, we didn't realize how much a stroll through the countryside, getting lost, would take it out of us. The thought of climbing the hill almost made us want to cry. But we'd walked all that way; it made no sense to stop now.

The climb was breathtaking (literally, for this out of shape college student). It was painful. We were huffing and puffing. The hill became slippery, and the wind picked up the further you climbed. About halfway up the hill, the path started to fade away, and the gradient became so steep we were afraid to go on.

Jackie had had enough and was going no further. But we'd walked all that way! I did the unchivalrous thing and left her behind (it was very cold in the B&B for the next few days). She stayed at a good spot to rest while I continued the climb, slipping and huffing and puffing my way up the hill. My muscles in my legs were on fire. I didn't have anything to drink and was incredibly thirsty.

And then something remarkable happened. I made it to the top. There was Melbury Beacon, the trig point. The view around me was the most incredible thing I'd ever seen. Melbury Hill was so high; I felt like

I was above the world. Dorset and Wiltshire surrounded me in a carpet of green rolling hills. Off in the distance, I could see a plane take off from Compton Abbas airfield.

As I snapped a million pictures, I heard footsteps and whispers as an elderly couple sauntered their way to the summit, having clearly taken an easier path from Compton Abbas.

"Lovely day for a walk," the old man said.

"Indeed, glorious weather for it," I responded.

My solitude at the summit over, I did the only sensible thing and headed back down the hill to my fuming fiancée.

Having had quite enough of getting lost and not wanting to do so on the way back, we noticed that the local bus would be stopping in a few minutes. So we did the most American thing ever and waited for the bus to let someone else drive us back to our B&B in Shaftesbury.

Having visited Shaftesbury a dozen times since that fateful walk, the irony is that I could now do that walk with my eyes closed, without a map. But the only way I was ever going to learn was to get lost in the process.

perfect moments. Everything was at peace. The dark blue night sky. The

The M&S Sandals

We'd arrived in Britain woefully unprepared. We didn't quite understand what English summer entailed. We didn't realize it was going to be so hot. So the first thing we had to do was go to Marks & Spencer, the British equivalent to Macy's, and buy some suitable summer attire.

One of the things I bought was a pair of sandals. I didn't give them much thought at the time, I just thought they would be perfect for the weather. I pretty much wore them for the rest of the trip. They were the perfect footwear for exploring the English countryside in the early summer of 2012.

I ended up having those sandals for five years. They were so comfortable and eventually my feet formed them into the perfect mould. Every summer here in the USA I would take them out and they'd still fit. They'd still be comfortable and last me the whole summer.

That is until they met a dog named Winston. One year we adopted a lab mutt and named him Winston (after Churchill, obviously). It took us a while to get to know him and change our habits around him. No shoe was safe. Not even my beloved 5-year-old M&S sandals. They made a delicious snack for his voracious appetite.

It was with a heavy heart that it was time to say goodbye to them and bury them (well toss them in the trash). Five years was a good run. Those M&S sandals were one of the best British buys I ever made.

When it came time to replace them, it made sense to return to Marks & Spencer. When I was in Britain for the Harry & Meghan Royal Wedding in 2018, I visited the M&S branch in Windsor, carefully rebranded 'Markle & Sparkle' for the occasion. Sure enough, I found the sandals in the men's section. They were slightly different but basically the same.

And expensive. They were £49! Quite a bit for a pair of sandals.

But I figured they were going to last me five years – that was just £10 a year.

And whenever I wear them, I'm reminded of my spiritual home.

Post-script.

Shortly after I initially wrote this short essay, Winston ate the new pair of M&S Sandals too. Don't worry, I still love Winston dearly and he still lives here. I ordered a replacement pair from M&S's website and had them shipped to the USA. They are safely stored in a drawer.

Visiting Tolkien's Grave
and Godstow Abbey

Come along with me on a lovely walk I took while I was staying in Oxford for a week. I was determined to go for at least one walk near Oxford while I was there. I really wanted to pay a visit to JRR Tolkien's grave in Wolvercote and then, when I discovered that not far from there is a ruined abbey along with a pub featured in the TV series Inspector Morse, the plan was sealed.

So on a sunny afternoon in July, I got a taxi to Wolvercote Cemetery and had one of the best experiences of my entire trip. I went for a walk. And it was a long walk, and I'm very glad I made myself do it. My life is generally very sedentary, I work from home, and now that it's winter, I don't get out much. So, one of the things I love the most when we make our trips to Britain is the chance to go for a walk in the countryside.

The taxi dropped me off right outside the gates to the cemetery. There were helpful signs along the way to point you to this special place. I've been a fan of Tolkien's works since I was a teenager so this was a pilgrimage I've always wanted to make. I practically had the cemetery to myself, which is an odd thing to be pleased about. I found the grave and smiled that other fans had adorned it with LOTR related stuff.

You'll notice that the gravestone says Beren and Luthien. This is a reference to a story from The Lord of the Rings about an elf-maiden who sacrifices her immortal life to be with the mortal man she loves. It's a beautiful and lovely story, and it was largely based on Tolkien's own love for his wife (which is an interesting story as she sacrificed much to be with him). Their gravestone is a monument to their love and the stories he created. If you're in Oxford and a Tolkien fan, I recommend stopping by this.

After I was done at the cemetery, I began my proper walk. At first I was walking through a residential neighborhood, and it wasn't really anything special. The roads were very busy. Wolvercote is basically a suburb of Oxford so many people who live there either work in Oxford or commute into London. I didn't encounter any people – it was late afternoon so everyone was at school or work! It was pleasant!

I began to cross Port Meadow. This is a large area of land, just north of Oxford, that has been common land since before William the Conqueror (1066). Commoners have the rights to graze their animals to this day. There are also allotments and walking paths. Standing on the railway bridge, you get expansive views of the whole of Port Meadow

below, and it's magnificent to behold. It's amazing to think that this land has been like this for so long and its history is so protected. I stood on that bridge for quite some time and watched the ant-like figures walk across the common. It was very peaceful and stunning to behold.

I like trains. I'm not a trainspotter, but I do like them a lot. This is the busy line in and out of Oxford, so there was a train going by every few minutes. I couldn't help but stand and wait for a few to go by. Coming from America and a busy area for trains, I was surprised at how fast the trains were moving – even the freight trains. Ours are so slow in comparison (and I know why).

As I was walking along the road into Wolvercote, I stumbled upon a beautiful pond that you wouldn't even know was there unless you looked closely. When I stood on the dock and gazed over its beauty, hidden away in a corner of Oxfordshire, I couldn't help but think I'd stepped into a children's storybook. I expected to see Peter Rabbit jumping into the water to go for a swim or Winnie the Pooh climbing a tree looking for honey. You can see why Tolkien was so inspired by the countryside surrounding Oxford.

The Trout Inn is a very popular pub on the River Thames. It's been featured in Brideshead Revisited and Inspector Morse (The Wolvercote Tongue episode). The building dates back to the 17th century. It's a bustling pub, but it wasn't too crowded when I visited on a Thursday afternoon. I was able to get a table. By this point, I'd walked almost 2 miles, so I was ready for a rest and a nice meal. This was the point of the trip when I missed my wife Jackie the most as she would have loved the waterside location.

Oddly, I found myself surrounded by lots of Americans. This pub is clearly popular with tourists. And that's fine. My meal was a lovely 28-day aged British Beef Rib-Eye steak and some glorious double cooked chunky chips. The meal was gloriously good pub grub and perfect after the long walk.

My view was of the ancient wood footbridge across the river. It's hard to believe that this little wooden bridge, which is a historical landmark and protected, spans the Thames, the same river that roars through London and into the sea. Here it's calm and relaxing.

I cannot resist visiting a ruined abbey so when I discovered Godstow Abbey, a former Benedictine nunnery, on my maps of Oxford, I knew I had to pay a visit. There's not much left other than the outline of the former monastery. Most of the building was sacked during the Dissolution of the Monasteries (thanks, Henry VIII, but it was also sacked during the English Civil War). It's quite amazing to find such a peaceful and abandoned ruin on the outskirts of a major city like Oxford.

Britain is full of places like these, and I love them to bits (I don't have many medieval ruins to explore in LaPorte, Indiana).

Finding places like this is always such a treat, especially when I have them all to myself. There was no one around so I could carefully compose my pictures to get the last golden sunlight just right. The ground was a bit treacherous and uneven, but it's so much fun to amble freely around an ancient ruin. Ruins like this are a bit odd – they just exist in the landscape. It's not a managed tourist attraction. You do not have to pay to get in, and there's no one minding it. Anyone can stumble across it and have a wander around and enjoy hundreds of years of history, completely for free. It's owned by English Heritage who look after the site, but they're pretty hands off.

Other than the walls around the former abbey, the ruined chapel is the only real structure left on the site. It's easy to imagine it finished with stained glass in the windows and a small group of nuns worshipping. I imagine it must have been very moving to worship here, especially when the sun was hitting the windows just right like it was when I visited.

I loved the windows that remained. The detail that has survived the ages is amazing. There's not much left on the rest of the site. The buildings of the monastery were plundered after the Dissolution and much of the stone was incorporated into many of the beautiful local cottages. If you want to see a monument to this long-gone institution, you simply have to look around Wolvercote, it's everywhere you look.

If you're in Oxford and a Tolkien and Morse fan, I highly recommend doing this walk. You will not regret it.

The Boat Ride to St Michael's Mount

I'd never been on the sea before. In twenty trips to the UK, I've only ever flown over the ocean, I've never been on it. The only boats I've been on have been on small lakes and on the Chicago River here in the American Midwest. It's not that I was afraid of it, or worried about seasickness, I just never had the chance. When we drove from Land's End to John O'Groats in 2018, I finally had the chance to go on the sea. And it was lovely.

Visiting St Michael's Mount had been on my 'bucket list' for almost as long as I'd been an Anglophile. That mysterious, quaint little island sitting in Mount's Bay, just outside Marazion in Cornwall. It's steeped in history and a very popular tourist attraction now managed by the National Trust, but still owned by the family that's always owned it. The kicker is that you can only get to the island one of three ways: on foot when the tide is low enough, by boat or by special amphibious vehicle. The day and time we visited, the only option was by boat.

The signs in Marazion direct you down to the seafront where's there's a stone weir that recedes into the bay. When the tide is low, you can go for a leisurely walk across the bay along a cobbled path. That day the tide was high and the bay was very choppy due to an oncoming storm. The island hadn't been closed yet. We watched as the first boat came across the bay, it appeared slowly, and then it was right in front of us. The boatmen helped everyone on board, and we paid our fare (it was £2, I believe, per person).

And with that, I was on a boat, on the sea. Well, if you count Mount's Bay as being the sea. Immediately it was like being on a roller coaster. The boatmen turned the boat around and pushed the throttle to its maximum and we began the crossing. Thankfully the boat was covered, otherwise we would have been soaked as the boat smacked into the waves as it crossed. Up and down. The noise was so loud, we could barely hear ourselves talk. Up and down. Up and down. Left and right. We occasionally smacked our bodies into the side of the boat. No one was brave enough to stand except the boatmen, whose legs were steady as tree trunks. Thankfully, I have a strong stomach and didn't get seasick.

The crossing took only ten minutes. It was rough. But it was fun. Halfway across I mentioned to Jackie that this was the first time I'd been on the sea and she was surprised – even after almost 20 years together, we still manage to surprise each other. It wasn't long until the water began to soften as we entered the sheltered harbor on St Michael's Mount. The

boat softly touched the harbor wall and we all climbed off. My legs were surprisingly steady. The crossing over had been exhilarating. But it was time for a cup of tea. And then the long hike up the mount to the castle.

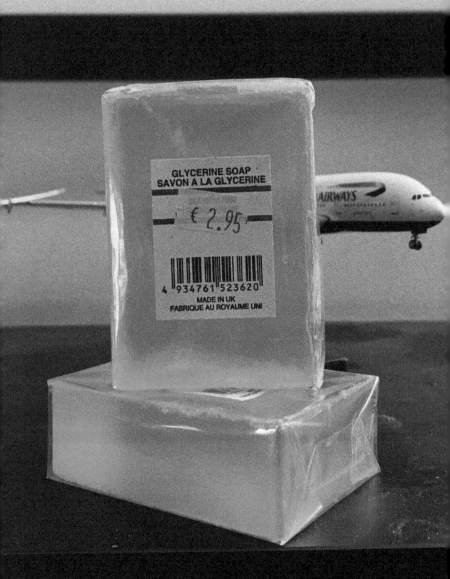

The Japanese Orange Soap

This is a story about soap. Japanese soap. I know, what does this have to do with Britain? Well, quite a bit, actually. You see, it's a soap I can only get in London and I only know about this soap because, on one of my first trips to London, British Airways lost our luggage.

It was our second trip to London as a couple (circa 2005), Mrs Anglotopia and I were not married yet (and Anglotopia was a good 4 years from existing). It was spring break and we'd been saving all year to go to London for our week off from college studies. Our classmates would go to Florida or Cancun for spring break, we went to London. Despite saving for almost a year, our budget was tight. We really had just enough money for our trip without much flexibility if anything went wrong.

So, of course, something went wrong. It's a particular kind of feeling, standing there in baggage reclaim, jet-lagged, waiting for your bag to come off the plane. And watching all your fellow passengers claim their bags to the point where the carousel is empty, and you realize that your bag is not coming off the plane.

After talking with customer service, it was clear that we would not get our bag back for at least 24-48 hours (they promised to deliver to our hotel). I was going to need a change of clothes, toiletries, etc. So we did the sensible thing and went shopping, hoping our meager funds would get us the basics. It was then that I came across Muji for the first time on Long Acre, just outside Covent Garden.

For those not familiar with it, Muji is a Japanese brand that focuses on minimalism and simple unbranded goods (well Muji is the brand but they don't put the name on it). They make the best pens for writing anywhere, so much so that anytime I let someone use a Muji pen, they immediately want to know where to get them. I came across their soap. They make a simple glycerin-based soap, injected with a scent. I loved the smell of the mandarin soap. It was the most wonderful orange smell. I bought a bar for our hotel shower.

And so I fell in love with this soap. Which is a weird thing to fall in love with. I have sensitive skin and it's the perfect soap and it smells like oranges, the best smell in the world. Pretty much on every trip since, I've gone to Muji and stocked up on pens, notebooks and orange soap (I usually buy at least 10 bars). I ration the soap, so it lasts as long as possible but, in the sometimes large gaps of time between trips to Britain, I inevitably run out. My skin does not like alternatives. So, I've gone to great lengths to get the soap. I once ordered it directly from Japan. Ordering it from the UK is not possible now, there's a workaround but it makes these simple bars of soap very expensive. Muji now has stores in the USA, but they do not sell the soap.

This soap has become part of my life and I don't want to live without it. When I open the soap and smell it, I'm immediately transported back to London in 2005. That feeling of endless possibility when you're still getting to know a new city, still falling in love with it. It's a reminder of all those early happy memories with Mrs Anglotopia. It's a reminder to myself that I must always go back to London because, if I don't, I will run out of soap.

A Bestselling Author's
Spit on My Leg

We had to walk around a fallen tree that hadn't and probably was never going to be cleaned up. The Cumbrian farmer, who was hosting the writers' retreat, was trying to 'rewild' his land and what better way to encourage that than force the footpath to go around a fallen tree? I pushed aside a branch to let some of the others in the group pass. And as I did so, my legs rubbed up against something.

Within seconds, I felt sharp pangs on my ankle which soon turned into an intense burning sensation. I got the attention of the farmer and said, "I brushed up against something and my leg is burning, should I be concerned?"

"Sounds like you met stinging nettles," he said. "Rub it with dock leaf. Mix them with your spit and rub them on your leg, that'll help."

He bent down to find a handful of dock leaves, which looked like a weed you wouldn't give a second thought to, ripped them from the plant and handed them to me. Slightly confused, I took the leaves and started to rub them together in my hands.

"No, like this," came another voice. It was the bestselling author who had also joined us on our walk up the fell (Cumbrian for mountain). He grabbed the leaves from my hand, then picked up even more and then said, "Excuse me, this'll be a bit strange."

He proceeded to spit into his hand quite a bit and rub together the leaves to release the soothing balm within. He then bent down and rubbed his wet hands, with the leaves inside on my leg. Having a famous author rub his spit all over my leg was not something I thought would happen when I woke up that morning.

They were right, though, after he spat into his hands some more and continued to rub deeply, the burning stopped. The farmer's old remedy was working. As I stood there with his hands on my leg, I found the whole scenario ironic. I was taken back to a few weeks before when I'd tried to read this chap's very well-regarded book. I threw it on the floor in annoyance.

"I'm not enjoying or getting this book," I said to my wife at the time.

"Then don't read it," she said. "Life's too short to read something you're not into."

"Then, I won't," I said. The next day I re-shelved the book.

I thought of that book, sitting in my library back home as he rubbed my legs. Here was an author, who didn't know me, genuinely helping me

and all I could think was that I didn't like his book.

Later on, I listened to him talk about his book and my interest was piqued again, so I reread the book when I returned home and I loved it. This wasn't something he ever would have known anything about, but I felt like I owed it to him for rubbing my leg with his spit; an unexpectedly intimate moment on a Cumbrian fell.

The Castle on the Busy Road

I generally have one rule when traveling in Britain; if there is a ruin near me, I will stop at the ruin. I love ruins. And Britain is full of them. Brougham Castle (pronounced 'Broom') is one of the finest castle ruins I've ever been to. Situated in the heart of Cumbria, next to a river, Brougham Castle is a quintessential Medieval castle ruin.

It was my final stop on a busy day of sightseeing. By this point on this hot summer day, I really didn't want to stop anywhere else. But it was a ruin. And I have to follow my own rules, otherwise what's the point in having them?

The castle is located next to a busy highway. I parked my car in the street and wandered along the road, stopping to look at the castle perfectly situated next to a busy river. The wind was blowing strongly that day, and the sound of the busy road next to the castle was very loud. This was not a peaceful, cloistered place like many other castle or cathedral ruins that I've been to.

The site is currently owned and managed by English Heritage, there is a small visitor center with artifacts found on the site along with a gift shop and a staff perfectly willing to help with guidance or history. The castle was founded by Robert I de Vieuxpont in the early 13th century. It's actually been 'ruined' twice in its history, for the final time in the 1700s. Now it's kept in stasis, with English Heritage seeking to keep it in its current form. When I was there, new cracks had appeared, necessitating a visit from a conservation expert.

The ruins are incredible. I pretty much had them to myself, save for a fellow American family that was eagerly exploring the place with a joy that only people who grew up in a country without castles can truly understand. At one point, my eagerness to see the place and take pictures felt like I was intruding on their adventure, so I tried to back off and let them experience the place on their own. There are plenty of other ruins on the grounds to explore. The view from the very top provided expansive views of the surrounding Cumbrian countryside.

While the setting is loud, and not peaceful, Brougham Castle is still very much worth a stop. The busy road makes it easy to find and get to (I've been to plenty of ruins that require getting lost on the way to gain entry…) You can see it in less than an hour so it's perfectly fine to visit on your way to somewhere else.

A Secret Place Where
Time Stands Still

No place with an entry in the official National Trust guidebook is truly a secret, but when you arrive at Calke Abbey in Derbyshire, you very much feel like you're passing into another realm and into the pages of a legend. This treasure of Britain's national heritage is kept in a state of 'arrested decay' as it was when it was given to the Trust in the 1980s. What resulted is a time capsule of 20th-century aristocratic decline and a truly special place, a secret place that we can all experience.

Arrival to Calke Abbey is down a long driveway, several miles in length. Past the gates to the estate, deep in the English countryside, you're given a CD by the security guard at the entrance. This CD tells you a story – it frames the secret place and it's perfectly timed to the drive along the single lane track, leading to the house. Only you have no idea the house is actually there. Amongst fallen trees and endless rolling green hills, it's difficult to tell if there is a house here at all. And you begin to wonder if the National Trust is pulling your leg.

Eventually you come around a bend and there it is, sitting in the landscape, a silent sentry to history. Calke Abbey stands on the site of a 12th-century Augustinian priory, and was built in the 1700s by the eccentric Harpur-Crewe family. It sits perfectly in the landscape and, for hundreds of years, the reclusive Harpur- Crewe family kept this view entirely to themselves, keeping the estate cut off from the world.

In their isolation, they filled the house with… well, the detritus that a family builds up for hundreds of years when it lives in the same building. This house is 100 Years of Solitude by Gabriel Garcia-Marquez in actual reality. Every room is packed to the gills with stuff. Most of it left as it was when the National Trust took over the house in the 1980s. The family came to the end of the line in the 1980s, their isolation no longer tenable in a house that was crumbling around them. In lieu of crippling death duties, they gave the house to the National Trust.

Normally when this happens, an army would descend upon the place and restore the house to its former glory, the way it was meant to be experienced in its golden age. They decided to do it differently with Calke Abbey. They decided to leave it as they found it. Walking through the house is to walk through a 300-year-old time capsule of English aristocracy. Rooms filled with random things, wallpaper peeling off the walls, paint chips on the ground. The whole place has the most wonderful smell, a combination of dust, leather and stale air. The clock

has stopped, the time machine has reached its destination. And now this is a place that we can enjoy, a sad, crumbling place that's a symbol of the decline of the British aristocracy in the 20th century. A sign in the café states that Calke Abbey is a 'secret place, where time stands still.' And it does.

Visit as soon as you can.

The
SHIP
TAVERN
EST. 1549
ALE HOUSE
&
DINING
ROOM

EST.
AL
DINING
ROOM

HOUSE &
549

BINET
RS OF
ALES
WORLD GIN
CABINET

My First, and Last, Pint

Turning twenty-one in America is usually a big deal. It signifies one major life change: you can now drink alcohol. And gamble. But alcohol is the big one. I was never really interested in alcohol but felt that the occasion of my twenty-first birthday elicited at least one drink. By this point in my life, I'd been to Britain three times. Each of those times, I could have taken a drink, if I'd wanted to. I'd been to enough pubs. I just wasn't interested.

But when it came time for my twenty-first, Jackie came up with the best idea.

"Why don't we go up to that English pub on the North side of Chicago," she said.

And so that's what we did. We lived about ninety minutes outside of Chicago, so a trek into the city was a Big Deal. We'd heard about this pub. It was supposedly the best English pub in the Midwest. The Red Lion was run by a tried and true Englishman. According to online reviews, it was decorated just as an English pub would be in London and served typically English fare like fish & chips and bangers & mash. As well as English brews.

It was also supposedly haunted.

We arrived in the afternoon, and it became clear that we were the only people there. Just us and the publican, who was indeed English. It was dark and smoky like you would expect to find a pub in England. There were typically English prints decorating the walls - Nelson at Trafalgar, pictures of the 1966 World Cup and various other bits of English ephemera, undoubtedly found in an antique mall somewhere in the Midwest. The publican told us how the bar itself came from England and was original. The seats looked like they were taken right out of an episode of Inspector Morse, hardwood with high backs.

I knew nothing about beer (I still don't). So, the publican suggested one and I said that'd be fine.

We sat down and ordered lunch. Being in 'full English' mode, I ordered fish & chips to go with my beer.

I liked that place. It really did feel a bit English, though it was easy to see that it was making a good imitation at being English. It's definitely the most 'authentic' British pub I've been to in the USA (most are dreadfully un-British - a Union Jack over the bar and Newcastle Ale on tap isn't what makes a British pub).

My beer arrived, and it was the moment of truth. It was a pint, a whole pint of Newcastle Brown Ale. I took a sip.

It was vile.

I practically spat it out.

"Beer is an acquired taste," said Jackie trying to suppress her laughter.

I truly hated it but thought the more I tried it, the more I might like it. I never liked it.

The fish & chips came, and I ordered a Sprite to wash them down. The fish & chips were very good but not authentic - fish strips and fuzzy over-fried fries are nowhere on the cricket pitch of authenticity.

So, we'd traveled all the way to Chicago. I hated the beer. The food wasn't great. But the pub was lovely. We never encountered the ghost, only my true distaste for alcohol. The pub is no longer there (though the name Red Lion lives on in other Chicago bars). And I sort of miss it.

But that was back in 2005. I still hate beer (I've tried several times since) and never drink alcohol. I'm well aware that drinking in pubs is a social pastime I'm missing out on. That's OK. You don't need to drink alcohol to appreciate the wonderfulness of pubs even though drinking is a big part of social life in Britain. You can feel left out sometimes. There have been several occasions where Brits have looked at me like I was from another planet when I order a soft drink in a bar. I just say I'm teetotal, and people usually leave it at that.

I still like British pubs, and you can still enjoy them without drinking. In fact, I would argue they're more enjoyable because you get to be the sober guy watching British people get drunk and amusing.

Travel Confessions of a Picky Eater

I hate trying new foods. I'm a ridiculously picky eater and have been my entire life. It caused my parents no end of frustrations. There were many incidents where I could not leave the table because I could not stomach something I was being fed, which led to the problem of having a visceral hatred of the things that I was forced to eat. Sorry, broccoli, I will never like you. You taste like farts.

This proved to be a problem when I started traveling to Britain. Because the food is different. Granted, there are many culinary similarities, but Britain has a completely different set of foods to try and eat. It also didn't help that my history with food was uncreative and focused on just what my parents could get me to eat. The problem with this is that on my early trips to England, I would spend my time there very hungry because the food was so different I barely ate.

This was unacceptable to Jackie, who took my inability to try new foods as a personal challenge practically from when we started dating (the bar was set very low, I took her to McDonalds on our first date - she's cringing reading this, isn't she?). It's a miracle I got a second date!

My early trips were a public service film in what not to eat when you go to Britain. I'd just find the American fast food. It was cheap, it was reliable, and I stayed fed. I'd eat McDonalds (which tasted different, but I could handle it). Pizza Hut. TGI Fridays. Then I'd branch out and eat at Britain's predictable chain restaurants like Garfunkels or Frankie and Bennies.

But as I got older, Jackie got to me. I was really missing out a huge part of travel in Britain by not being adventurous and trying new foods. British food is fantastic, anyone that tells you otherwise has attitudes towards Britain that are too dated to be worth listening to. So I've made it a point to try things and slowly, over 15 years of travel, I've tried lots of British food. I've found some things I hate. I've found some things I love. But most of all, I'm proud that I'm more willing to try new things.

When you first think of British food, you immediately think of fish & chips. It's a staple of the British diet. Every town has a chippy (a place where you can buy fish & chips). Most are greasy and horrible. Some are not. But I've tried fish & chips several times over the years, and I still cannot abide it. I just don't like fish and, no matter how much I try it, I cannot acquire a taste for it. I'll eat it in a pinch and just focus on the battered goodness, but I'm not going to go out of my way to get fish & chips. Chips, however, are another matter. Because without trying fish

& chips, I never would have realized how amazing British chips are. Chunky chips are a gift from the gods. I'm salivating as I'm writing this. So, the good thing about chippies is that they don't just have fish, most fry chicken as well. So, a perfect hearty British dinner for Jackie and me is her getting fish & chips (which she loves), and I'll get chicken & chips. So good.

Growing up, I was never a big fan of roast beef. It wasn't even a meal my mother made in our home. But then I'd never had British Sunday Roast. Sunday Roast is a great British tradition, and you must have it in a country pub somewhere. When I tried it for the first time and then learned how important Sunday Roast was in the British social calendar, it became a must-do for all of our trips. We always book into a pub for Sunday Roast now (and you have to book a place in the best pubs, or you won't find anywhere that can seat you). Sunday Roast can vary between beef, lamb, or chicken. I always opt for the beef. Getting a plate full of roast beef, with the veggies and potatoes, all drowned in gravy (which I never used to like) is culinary ecstasy. But it's one of those things I never knew I liked until I tried it in Britain.

We've had our share of food disasters. Once, we were dining with friends in a very nice restaurant on the Thames that was known for steak. I'm one of those terrible Americans that likes his steak well-done (though recently, I've softened to medium-well). When I told the waiter I wanted my steak well done, he looked at me with horror and said, "But sir, our chef will only cook steak blue." Not knowing what that meant and not wanting to be embarrassed in front of our friends, I said that was fine.

When the steak came, I learned what blue meant.

It means it's basically not cooked. Essentially, it's run through a warm room.

Our friends were buying, so I put on a brave face and ate as much of that uncooked steak as I could manage.

Another British mainstay that I've learned to love is a meat pie. We don't really do meat pies here in the States though pot pies are popular. I never really liked pot pies. Pies are for fruit. You don't put meat in a pie. Well, the British do, and it's amazing. When I tried a hot beef pie for the first time, I was pleasantly surprised at how much I loved it. Now, whenever I get the chance, I try to get a meat pie.

When we were traveling in Cornwall, I knew I couldn't leave without trying a Cornish Pasty, the local variation on a meat pie. I was quite nervous about trying it but, as I'd liked other British meat pies, I was ready to give it a go (to borrow a British phrase). When I bit into that pasty for the first time (along with my serving of chips), it really cemented in me that the reason the British stuff all this food into pies is because it's delicious. I loved my first Cornish pasty, and I can't wait to have another.

In Scotland I tried Haggis. They don't let you leave the country unless you try their cherished national dish. I'll be honest, I didn't love it. And when you describe to me what Haggis is, it just... sounds disgusting. I can understand why the USA bans its importation. It was tasty. But knowing what it's made of and how it's made, I'm going to take a permanent hard pass on that dish. Sorry, Scotland.

Jackie is probably reading this chapter and laughing. I don't want this to sound like I've been cured of my picky and unadventurous eating. I most certainly have not. I've just managed, kicking and screaming, to try new foods, slowly over 15 years. I've found some things I liked and found some things that I don't like and will never eat again. But I'm very glad my picky eating habits have improved. And so is Jackie. Sometimes on our trips, I don't eat any fast food at all. But sometimes, when you're on the road for 6 hours, and you haven't had lunch, it's perfectly all right to stop at McDonalds and eat the worst food you can order. And to have your wife eat it along with you.

Then that night eat a gourmet dinner.

On the Train from
Windsor to Slough

Windsor has two railway stations. One of them isn't very grand but has several hourly connections to London's Waterloo Station. The other station is a much grander place, but long ago stopped being a major train station - it's now mostly shops and cafés - save for a single remaining platform. It provides a five-minute connection to Slough Station, a major junction where you can connect to pretty much anywhere in England. When you're in Windsor you'll likely want to take a fast train to London or Oxford.

But this little five-minute journey from Windsor & Eaton Central is a remarkable thing in itself. It runs every twenty minutes, like clockwork, your single carriage goes from Windsor to Slough, along a route that features incredible views of the countryside. It's a single track, just two miles long. The journey goes by in a blink, but it's a wonderful journey.

On the way to Slough, you get lovely views of the countryside surrounding Windsor. You can see Eaton off in the distance. There are footpaths, and you often see people walking on them. Airplanes fly over on their approaches to Heathrow. Slough is much bigger than Windsor, so you see it looming in the distance.

On the way back from Slough to Windsor, it's a completely different view. You get to watch this beautiful, ancient town (over 1,000 years old!) come into view. The views of the castle are worth the train ticket alone. It's especially beguiling at night when the castle is lit up like a Christmas tree.

The ride is fast but you kind of want it to go on forever as you amble and bounce either to or from Windsor. The two stations could not be more different. Windsor & Eaton Central is a stately old railway station, long ago bypassed by other lines. It's lucky to even have a single train still running to it. The rest of the place is lovingly cared for and a center of commerce with plenty of shops and restaurants. It's basically a railway-themed mall (what's not to like about that?). Slough, however, lives up to its reputation from the UK version of The Office. It's a very functional station, designed to move people quickly around. It's old, but not stately like Windsor & Eaton, rather it shows its age, and it's rather a challenge to get around.

But thanks to the frequency of trains along the Great Western Railway, you never really have to linger there for very long. The wonders of England's railways await you. Whether you're venturing off to the

West Country or taking a fast train into London, your journey starts at a quaint little station in Windsor & Eaton. And it's always a nice one to return too. It's only a few minutes long, but it's one of Britain's best train journeys.

Old and New Wardour Castle

Shaftesbury in Dorset is the closest place we have to a hometown in England when we visit. We've stayed there almost a dozen times over 15 years of travels so we've got to know the place like we have our own place back home. As with most small towns in England, there is a local 'castle.' Shaftesbury has a ruined castle and quite a few stately homes, but two are the most famous of all: Old Wardour Castle and New Wardour Castle (which are actually in Wiltshire, not Dorset). Before a trip a few years ago, I found a lovely walk that took in the old castle and then took you on a walk through the Dorset countryside to the new 'castle' (it's a stately home, not a castle). It's just over three miles, and it was great.

Old Wardour Castle probably looks familiar to you and that's because it was used in the film Robin Hood, Prince of Thieves (the one with Kevin Costner and a Robin Hood with an American accent). It's a hexagonal castle, modeled after a French style, and is actually the only one in England. It's been a ruin since just after the English Civil Wars. It was seized by Parliamentary forces and taken over, then taken over again by the Royalists. It never recovered.

Neighboring New Wardour Castle was then built in the Palladian style (more on this later). The ruin was left as an ornamental part of the new estate's gardens, and it remains such to this day. The castle is currently owned and managed by English Heritage. The castle was closed on the day of our walk (so visit on a day when you can go in and check it out). It's usually only open at weekends in the winter, so we could not have a look around (we'd had a look around back in 2012, it's great, you should go). While the castle was closed, the car park was still open, and the estate walk on public footpaths was open as well.

The walk starts at the Old Castle car park, which is where we parked our rental car. I was a bit disappointed the castle was closed but, as we'd seen it before, we didn't feel we were missing out. I was really interested to see how it sat in the Wardour estate landscape. You get but a peek of the castle from the walk as you begin. I love romantic old castle ruins. It's a simple love. The castle was ruined during the English Civil Wars, during that period almost no part of England was untouched.

Along the way we came across a beautiful Dorset shepherds' hut. They're very much a part of the landscape in 'Wessex.' They used to be where the shepherds lived while they tended their flocks of sheep. There's a very famous scene in Far from the Madding Crowd by Thomas

Hardy where Farmer Oak almost dies in his hut and is rescued by Bathsheba Everdene. They've fallen out of use as actual shepherds' huts but now it's in vogue to have one on your property as a 'man cave' or office. David Cameron, former UK Prime Minister, famously put one in his back garden to write his memoirs (which I suspect few people actually wanted to read). There are companies that specialize in building these now – I'd love to have one built and shipped to the USA to be placed in the 2 acres of woods on our property in Indiana. Must buy a lottery ticket!

As you proceed down a muddy lane you're given glimpses of New Wardour Castle. Just as we walked by, we were blessed with golden, low winter sunlight shining directly onto the house. This Palladian-style house sits triumphantly in the landscape. I could not stop gazing at it. Despite the distance, I took far too many pictures. We also realized at this point that this walk was perhaps a bit longer than we intended as the route would take us to that house and back.

As estates are reconfigured or changed through the ages, you'll find old gates sitting orphaned in the English countryside. This one was particularly pretty, and the muddy path makes it seems like you're stepping back in time. It's easy to stand back and imagine a carriage running through the arch, on its way to call on a lady at a grand stately home. The details that have survived the ravages of time and continuous Wiltshire winters is astounding. I would not be surprised if this structure is actually listed and protected.

I'm always amazed at how green the English countryside is in the dead of winter. Back home in Indiana, everything has a brown hue (or in our case when we were there, blinding white) to it. England stays gloriously green year-round. We were on a public footpath, but this 'public' path crossed private land. These old rights of way sometimes date back hundreds of years. One went right through a farmer's field, and we had hundreds of sheep for company. They completely ignored us. We were very interested in them as Jackie is an avid knitter. She would love to steal their wool! But the first rule of walking in the English countryside is: do not disturb livestock. They continued to amble the hill and eat grass, and we continued our walk.

Despite being February, it was actually pretty warm the day we did this walk. It was in the 40s and 50s (°F) that day. One reason we love Dorset and Wiltshire so much is that its location relative to the coast keeps it warmer through the winters. Jackie always looks her best ambling in the English countryside with me.

We were losing our sunlight. But that was expected. The clouds move so fast in the winter sometimes that you can have multiple moments of golden sun and gloom within the space of an hour. After this point, we walked through a beautiful ancient wood. For some reason, I didn't take a picture of it, and I wish I had. As we walked through the forest, there was a roar of sound, which was odd in the countryside where it's usually so quiet, and all you can hear is the birds (even in the winter). I suspected there was a road nearby, but even with my basic knowledge of the era, I knew there was not.

"What is that noise?" I asked somewhat rhetorically to Jackie.

"It's the trees," she responded.

I looked up, and she was right. The roar was not a nearby road – it was the winds blowing through the trees in this sheltered valley. We stopped and listened. It was a marvelous sound. It sounded like England's ancient history calling out to us. I imagined warriors hiking through this forest. Shepherds droving their flocks to the next field. Victorian lovers stealing a kiss away from the public eye.

At one point in the walk, I managed to get stuck in the mud and fall down at which point Jackie made quite a bit of fun at my expense. Minutes later she took a tumble into the mud herself. The teasing ceased. We were now both covered in mud but having so much fun. Also, this just proved that wellies are essential for any walk in the English countryside, especially in the winter. They take up a lot of room in your suitcase, but you need them in situations like this! Because you will inevitably have to wade into muddy tracks like this! Easy to get stuck and fall. Proper foot attire is essential.

It's so weird, the route we were on took us right through a farmer's yard (houses, barns, equipment). It's a public right of way, but it still feels so odd to walk right through the middle of someone's property. Thankfully we didn't encounter anyone, so there was no real awkwardness. Once we left the farmyard (I respectfully didn't take pictures despite it being beautiful), we followed the path along a fence and were treated to more views of New Wardour Castle and celebrated the return of the sun.

As we walked along the fence towards our destination, a runner came up from behind us. He was happy to chat. He was doing the same route – he lived nearby and used the public right of way for his daily runs. We had questions about the route, and he knew exactly which way we needed to go. He ran off, and we watched him incredulously as he ran up the hills ahead of us, seemingly with no effort. We were at least in mile 2 of our walk by this point and were very sore and exhausted. We don't get to walk much like this when we're back home and are out of shape. The idea of running this route so effortlessly made us tremble with fear.

Finally, we arrived at New Wardour Castle. We'd never been this

close to it before. The public footpath literally takes you through the back garden. This house is not open to the public, ever. It's privately owned. But not by some rich Lord & Lady. The house was sold off years ago to a developer who turned the house into flats and townhouses (very expensive flats and townhouses, I should add). You can get the thrill of living in a stately home for a fraction of the price and upkeep.

The only bit of the house that's open to the public, other than the footpath, is the Catholic Chapel inside, which is regularly open for Sunday services. I would very much like to see this chapel sometime. There is also a very famous rotunda staircase that's architecturally important, but not something you can see unless you're a resident. There are ten apartments inside. The stable blocks were also turned into apartments. The presence of cars parked in the front made it difficult to photograph this beautiful house but at the end of the day, you have to realize that this is a small community of people – not a grand stately home open to the public. It's like a village, but in a stately home instead.

The landscape around the house had been sculpted for the pleasure of the original owners. The gardens went through several iterations – including one by the renowned landscape architect Capability Brown who undertook extensive earth moving and tree planting between 1775 and 1783. His work is largely what you see today.

Old Wardour Castle was kept as a landscape ornament as part of the new parklands around the house, and it's at this point that you can start to see it again. Getting back to the old castle is a much shorter walk from New Wardour Castle than the long circuitous route we took through the countryside. But it was so very much worth it to see New Wardour Castle, sitting in the landscape designed by Capability Brown, occasionally bathed in golden, low winter sunlight.

On the Ullswater Steamer

I arrived at Pooley Bridge with about 30 minutes to spare. I figured that was plenty of time to catch the next steamer to Glenridding. I parked in the car park for Pooley Bridge as that's where the postcode that Ullswater Steamer's brochure provided sent me.

There was a hiccup when the machine in the car park wouldn't take my money. But it wouldn't take anyone's money. The machine was out of order, and this was a scenario I haven't encountered before in England. A young woman also trying to park simply said, "Just leave a note on your dashboard that the machine doesn't work."

That's what I did and as I walked away I hoped that I didn't return a few hours later to a parking fine on my windscreen. I've prided myself in that, over the ten years I've been driving in the UK as a tourist, I've never gotten a speeding ticket or traffic fine of any kind. I did not want this day to be the first time for that.

This is where clueless traveler comes in. I didn't know where to catch the Ullswater Steamer from Pooley Bridge. There was a sign in the car park with the sailing times. But there was no sign indicating where you catch the boat or which direction to walk. I walked towards the center of the village, and still, no signs there indicated anything. I looked across Pooley Bridge and saw people walking, but no sign indicating the boats were in that direction.

Finally, I saw lots of people coming down a drive.

That must be it, I thought. They must be streaming in from the lake.

I began to walk down the drive, and as I got to a turn, I began to wonder if I was heading to the wrong place.

"Is this the way to the boat?" I asked some random English person walking past.

"No, mate," he said. "It's back over the bridge about 100 meters down the street.

"Thank you," I responded.

I backtracked to the bridge. I followed the pavement along the road. There were lots of people headed in the same direction, so I felt confident that I was heading in the right direction. I looked at my phone, and I was running out of time.

I walked, and I walked — way more than 100 meters.

Where the heck was this thing? I wondered, starting to sweat in the mid-afternoon heat.

Finally, I came around a curve in the street and saw the ticket office for the Ullswater Steamers and then eventually the boat came into view. And there was a crowd around it. Apparently, on this beautiful day, many people had the same idea as me.

My first thought was that there's no way I could get a spot on that boat with a decent view as it sailed along the lake. I went into panic mode. Should I chuck it in and cancel this? I'd already walked all this way. I was exhausted. I was hot. It would be cool on the boat. I could sit on the boat. For two hours.

I sighed and went into the ticket office and bought a return ticket (£15.95). I was very thirsty, and they were out of water bottles. I was so hot, I was starting to feel slightly queasy, which is not something you want to feel when you're about to get on a boat for two hours. I was regretting my decision to skip lunch and just have cake at that National Trust property I'd visited previously. I purchased a soda and a bag of chips, hoping that eating something, anything, would tide me over for the boat ride.

I walked quickly along the long, white wooden dock. My ticket was checked, and I stepped aboard. My plan was to record the journey using my GoPro, so I could share it later on. The best place to do this would be the front of the boat. So I went downstairs and walked through the boat to get to the bow. Thankfully, there was still a space I could fit in. I set up my camera, attaching it to the railing on the hull.

We pulled away shortly thereafter, I ate my bag of chips and drank my soda, and I immediately felt better. It was hot, and the sun was beating down on the open deck. But once the boat turned around after clearing the dock and began to steam across the lake, we were treated to a cool breeze.

Ullswater is the longest of the lakes, but it's only about 9 miles long (and at most 3/4 of a mile wide). The steamer takes the better part of an hour to make the entire journey. But, despite this, the boat feels like it's going pretty fast. The bow was somewhat crowded as people jostled to get a view of the surrounding landscape and take pictures as we went along.

As with most travel experiences like this in Britain, I was the youngest person on the boat. This always bothers me. It's a bit sad that there aren't more people my age out exploring and experiencing sublime things like this; most people my age are cooped up in offices working. Another reminder of how truly lucky I am to be able to experience Britain on my own terms and write about it.

Ullswater Steamers have been plying the tourist trade on the lake for more than 150 years. All of their boats run on steam engines, some were built in the Victorian Age, some are newer. The boats run a regular schedule for 363 days of the year. It's something you can rely on. Many people take the boat for part of the way, then walk part of the way, then get the boat again (they have tickets that accommodate this). The trip has no commentary (though if you download their mobile app, you can get commentary).

To be honest, there's not much to commentate on as the boat sails across the lake. There is nothing of real interest other than the beautiful landscape that surrounds you. Ullswater is very undeveloped, and this is by design. There are no great houses along the lake, no large towns or buildings to look at. No, the landscape is the star, and that's what you've paid £15.95 to look at.

My stomach settled once I had eaten my snack and rehydrated. As the journey progressed out deep into the water, the heat began to get worse. While there was a breeze as the boat steamed through the lake, the harsh midday sun was relentless. The front of the boat was a bit crowded, and we all jostled for position to take pictures as we passed particularly pretty parts of the landscape. No one was rude about it though; we were all there for the same reason - to capture a moment from something spectacular.

For most of the journey to Glenridding, I sat and soaked in the view, occasionally taking a picture if I saw something pretty. I also monitored the GoPro just to make sure it was doing its job. It was amazingly quiet out on the water, just the sound of the steam engine chuffing away. There were many others out enjoying the beautiful day on the lake, quite a few sailboats and groups of people learning how to sail.

There were also groups of Boy Scouts on the shore, climbing cliffs and jumping off. I felt rather jealous. The most exciting thing I got to do as a Boy Scout was to go to a summer camp for a week. These scouts got to jump into an Alpine-like lake. I was sweating profusely and jumping in the lake sounded like a very good idea at that moment.

Then the boat came to a stop. We were approaching our stop at Howetown (what a remarkable name for a place). A sister ship was currently in the dock, so we had to wait our turn. As the breeze stopped because the boat was not moving, the heat started to build. Jumping in the water began to look attractive. After a few moments, the sister ship got underway, heading towards Pooley Bridge where we'd just come from. Our engine fired up again, this time slowly as we chuffed into the dock.

"You have to move!" barked one of the crew at me, so I hurriedly moved my GoPro setup because the crewman needed to access the ropes and cast on to the dock.

Several people got off, quite a few got on.

Then the engine fired on again.

"Arms! Arms! Arms!" shouted the crewman at everyone in the front of the ship as we quickly moved backward along the dock. Fair enough. It could easily have chopped off a finger or dislocated an arm.

After Howetown, we rounded a mountain, and the view changed to a new vista. I really could not believe that such a landscape was real, let alone that I was there to see it in person. I've seen so many pictures of the Lake District; but none of that prepares you for actually seeing it in person. To visit the Lakes is to be in awe during your entire visit.

In no time at all we arrived at Glenridding, the other main terminus for the Ullswater Steamers. Everyone got off the boat. The journey back would be in 15 minutes. Glenridding has a completely different vibe than Pooley Bridge, which felt a bit like a tourist trap. Glenridding was more sedate. The car park was full of cars, and the beaches around the area were filled with sunbathers and people going for a swim.

I'd planned to GoPro the journey back, but my flash card was full. And your correspondent failed to bring a spare because he thought one was plenty. I thought perhaps that the gift shop on the dock would have one, but they didn't. The chap inside recommended going into the village, but I didn't have the time, and I didn't want to miss the boat back.

Well, I kind of did. I actually pondered just taking a taxi back to Pooley Bridge. I didn't relish getting on the boat again. I'd 'done' it; I'd filmed it. Got plenty of pictures. I wasn't too keen on getting back on the boat with it being so hot.

"Ridiculous," I told myself. "At least do it because you paid for a return ticket."

Sod it.

I got back on the boat.

This time, though, I managed to get a seat under the shaded canopy. This would hopefully make for a much cooler ride back. At first, I sat against the funnel but was surprised to feel how warm it was. Proof that the thing was actually run by a steam engine.

I relocated to a different spot, ate a snack and drank something I'd picked up in the dock gift shop. This journey would not be recorded by the GoPro. So I did what was exceedingly difficult to do. I just sat there and took in the scenery as the boat got underway. I tried to practice some mindfulness tips and truly relish being in such a wonderful place. I did nothing on the boat ride back. My mind was quiet. I was at peace.

I was pleased to see that the boat takes a different route back to Pooley Bridge, along the northern shore of the lake (it sometimes stops at the Aira Force National Trust park - but that day would not). I was really surprised at how different the view was and how different the lake

felt.

By this point, it was very late afternoon. The whole boat was snoozy. Even the rambunctious children were pretty sedate. The old English gentleman across from me, with a very friendly black lab on a leash, dozed off for most of the journey. One could not help but get a bit sleepy.

The journey reminded me of my honeymoon with Jackie. We'd decided to go to Lake Geneva, Wisconsin, a special place for us as we visited many times before we married. Despite having visited Lake Geneva so many times, we'd never done the steamer boats that ply that pseudo-Alpine lake that's so popular with Chicago tourists. So, on our honeymoon, with not much else to do, we decided to do it. The journey was similar in length to my journey on Ullswater, but it was cold and rainy (we got married in October). The commentary told us all about the rich people who lived (or had lived) in the mansions along the lakeshore.

Most of the Ullswater lakeshore was either part of the National Park or owned by the National Trust. It was open for anyone to enjoy. There is, in fact, a footpath that goes around the entire lake. Judging by the mountains surrounding it, this could be quite strenuous.

But most of all, this journey made me miss Jackie, my usual travel partner in crime who was back home in Indiana and unable to join me on this trip. She would have loved the mountains and the sailboats whizzing across the lake.

The boat once again made a stop at Howetown and then resumed the journey back to Pooley Bridge. It felt as if the boat was going faster this time. I was grateful, despite enjoying the stunning views, I really didn't want to be on the boat anymore. And my regular camera battery had died (guess who didn't bring the spare battery - you'd think I was an amateur at this!).

Soon enough, the boat docked and we all shuffled off, beginning the long walk back to Pooley Bridge car park. I'd had a busy day before the boat ride, and now I was properly knackered. When I returned to my car, exhausted from the voyage and the walk back to the car, I was pleased to see there wasn't a parking ticket on the windscreen. It felt like a minor victory worth celebrating.

I climbed in and called Jackie. I needed to talk to her. And I did for at least 30 minutes before the mountains around Ullswater cut off the signal.

Lake Geneva has been ruined for me. Ullswater is a 'proper lake.' I must come back to Ullswater, and next time with Jackie so we can rent a sailboat and spend a day on the water. Hopefully on a day that is not nearly as hot.

Paying My Respects to Winston

It's a strange thing to want to pay my respects to a man who's been dead for fifty years. But when I visited Churchill's birthplace at Blenheim Palace, it seemed only fitting to make an effort to go down the road and visit the place where he's buried. I don't know what I was expecting from the experience, but I wanted to see the place where my biggest hero was resting for eternity.

Most of the Churchill family are buried in their ancestral plot in the churchyard of St Martin's in the village of Bladon, located next to the Blenheim Estate. We found the village easily enough on our way to Blenheim but finding somewhere to park was a different matter entirely. We must have circled the town four times looking for a suitable place to park. You can't park at the church itself as it isn't allowed.

Luckily we found parking down a side street. There's a pub car park nearby as well – you're not supposed to park there unless you're a customer, but we saw plenty of people do it. It's not like you'll be at the grave for a long time. It was early enough in the day so I don't think anyone would have been bothered wherever we ended up parking.

The graveyard is a little bit of a trek up a hill, and you come up from behind. The yard would be a quiet, contemplative place if we hadn't gone during recess time at the school next door. Still, it's a beautiful setting for the grave of one of history's greatest men.

The grave is rather understated for a man of his importance. A simple stone slab marks his resting place. When I visited it was looking rather worn but apparently, since I visited, it's been spruced up a bit. There's no statue or massive tomb like other famous British warriors such as Nelson or Wellington. There are plenty of statues of Churchill elsewhere. Still, the plain stone burial plot is a moving tribute to the man; there's usually wreaths or flowers lying on the grave (feel free to bring your own). Many of the people he played a role in rescuing regularly leave flowers. A world forever grateful.

I paid my respects to someone I admire greatly. It's really something that meant a lot to me – as lame as it sounds.

After that, we went into the little church where they have a few things for sale on the honor system (leave the money in the box). I bought a few Churchill mementos and then we were on our way. The church itself is rather charming, and it takes great pride as the stewards of Churchill's grave. The proceeds from the honesty shop go to maintaining the graveyard.

When you go, we recommend visiting at a weekend, there's a school next to the cemetery and it's rather noisy so, if you want to pay your quiet respects, during the school day is not the time. The cemetery is open daily. There's no charge but feel free to leave a donation in the church so they can continue to maintain the grave. I suppose you can walk from Blenheim if you were so inclined, but it'd be a rather long walk.

It's a reminder that, no matter our impact on the world, we all end up in the same place, buried in the ground. The memories of most people are forgotten after a generation or two. The memories of history's greatest figures will endure for eternity. 100 years from now, people will still visit Winston's grave. 200. 300. What a legacy.

A Changing Heathrow

When I arrived at Heathrow Airport on my first trip to Britain in 2001, I was not impressed. The airport was over capacity even then, and our plane arrived late, so we had no gate for the plane to park at. We parked out on the tarmac, far away from the terminal. We had to queue for a bus, which then took us on a circuitous route to the terminal. While parking on the tarmac gave me the moment of literally stepping onto English ground for the first time, I couldn't help but think there was a better way for an arrival.

The terminal wasn't a much better experience. It was the old Terminal Two (since demolished), and it was showing its age. Built in the 1970s, it was dark, dirty and not fit for purpose. It felt like arriving into the past, and not the good past we imagine in England, but the past with terrible architecture and public spaces. The terminal was not the welcome you were expecting of 'Cool Britannia' when you arrived at Heathrow. For years afterwards when I heard Brits grumble about how terrible Heathrow was, I understood why they felt that way.

I experienced the omnishambles of Heathrow fully on my next trip in 2004. We arrived early on an overnight flight. Really early. The tailwinds pushed us to Britain so quickly that we arrived before Heathrow was even open and allowed to let planes land. We had to circle for a good 45 minutes until we could. This is pretty common coming into Heathrow because the airport is at capacity and landing slots are scarce. We hate, hate, hate circling. It makes my stomach do somersaults.

And when we landed this time, we didn't have a gate.

So we had to bussed, yet again, to the terminal, which was just as dark and dirty as I remembered from 2001. We were tired. I cannot sleep sitting up on an overnight flight so by my clock it was late or early depending on how you want to think of that fluid concept of time. We waited at baggage arrival for our bags to arrive.

And waited.

Jackie's bag showed up in due course. But after all the bags had arrived and were claimed, the conveyor built stopped, and I stood there, not quite understanding what it all meant. Then I realized that my bag had never showed up, it was lost. We wandered over to the customer service desk, and I remember it being a particularly dark and dungeon-like area of the terminal and got our first great experience of indifferent British customer service.

I can't blame the person. His entire job was to deal with people

angry that their bags were missing. And I must admit that we were very American about the situation, which I'm sure irritated him no end, we were very young. He did some searching in the ancient computer (which looked like something out of the 80s film Wargames) and sighed.

"It's in my system, it's in the airport somewhere, just not here. Give me your mobile number, and we'll contact you when it arrives."

No indication of when that could be. We grumbled and left the airport. It felt weird to have no luggage with me. All I wanted was a change of clothes. Once we'd checked into our hotel, we wandered over to Marks & Spencer in Covent Garden and bought a change of clothes and other essentials to tide us over until the bag showed up. Being poor college students, this did not please me.

The bag did eventually show up at the hotel the next day, thankfully. British Airways were kind enough to hand deliver it at no extra charge.

The next few trips would be a bit of a blur when going through Heathrow. You would just treat it as a place to pass through and I wasn't impressed with Arrivals. We usually departed from a nicer terminal, which had something alien to us, traveling from Chicago - shops, and restaurants. It was basically a shopping mall inside an airport. At the time, when you departed Chicago O'Hare's International Terminal, there was almost nothing beyond the gates (this has since changed).

Then I began to hear whispers of something new.

Something called Terminal Five.

Heathrow Terminal Five was Britain's biggest construction project at the time. In the works for almost 20 years, it was under construction for nearly a decade. On some of those early trips, you could see the construction site on the far west end of Heathrow when you taxied during arrivals and departures. And slowly, a soaring metal structure began to take shape. Terminal Five was to be dedicated completely to British Airways traffic. As we always flew BA, this was exciting.

When Terminal Five opened fully in 2008, it was a disaster. The state-of-the art baggage system failed. People went to the wrong gates. It was a massive screw up and national embarrassment, further fuel for the naysayer brigade in Britain who think they can never do anything right. It took them a few months to work out the kinks, but they did.

By the time I traveled through Terminal Five for the first time in 2009, everything was working smoothly. I remember arriving early in the morning from a chartered British Airways flight, and we parked right at the terminal gate. What joy! There was no bus. As I exited the plane, we were met with fresh air, the place still smelled new. The tile floors were gleaming. It felt like what an airport should be. As we snaked through escalators to the immigration line, it was such a nice experience.

We even got through immigration quickly. And in the gleaming new baggage hall our bags arrived promptly.

Then we got the special treat of getting access to a place we'd never even heard of, the Arrivals Lounge. It was a magical place where you could decompress after your flight. You got a full, free, hot breakfast, all you could eat. There were showers and bathrooms to freshen up. Massages. TV. And more free British newspapers than you can shake a stick at. It was glorious.

When we departed the next week we were presented with the full stunning effect of the terminal when we saw its single span roof for the first time (the largest in Europe). The terminal was so open and massive. What really surprised me was how quiet it was, despite its size and the number of people in it. Every time I've gone through Terminal Five since I always marvel at what a remarkable structure it is. We always get through Security in less than five minutes. The sooner to funnel you through the mall of shops and restaurants on the other side. The more time you spend there, the more money you can spend.

And Terminal Five has very nice lounges. On one occasion we got to go into the Concorde Room (the one for First Class). We were waited on hand and foot. It was such a quiet and warm environment with free computers to use, free food and drinks, and even free massages. When we sat down to lunch in the proper restaurant (that was included in the ticket) we, of course, got the best service. And we were giddy as schoolchildren when Piers Morgan sat down at the table next to us with his family, flying off to America as well. The closest I've ever been to a celebrity. While Piers Morgan has a reputation, many of the British people hate him (they have a similar disregard for James Corden as well), he was perfectly nice to everyone in the lounge that day, so I don't have anything bad to say about the man.

Traveling through Heathrow Terminal Five, even when you don't get to go into the lounge, is quite a contrast to what it was back in 2001. It's a proper welcome and goodbye from England. I've traveled through T5 a dozen times now, and I love every moment I get to spend there. I really love sitting down and watching planes take off and land on both sides of the terminal. It's easy for air travel to be terrible, all it takes it one small aspect for the system to fail - whether it's a lost bag, delay or cancellation. But going through Terminal Five is how air travel should start and end. It's set a standard now. A standard that has moved to other terminals at Heathrow as they've been closed, torn down and replaced.

It helps if you have routines when you go through the airport. I always eat at the same restaurant before boarding. We always hit the same duty-free shops to stock up on tea and biscuits before coming home. We always stop by at Hamleys and pick up a toy for each of our children. I must pick up a couple of British newspapers for the plane. I must buy a big bottle of water (I get very dry flying) along with real European-made Haribo gummy bears (which are superior to the ones made at home). I must also visit the WH Smith and see if there are any books worth getting as there is usually a 3 for 2 deal going on. And then once we have a gate, it's time to sit and wait to board our flight. The Terminal is always clean, always quiet.

It's not a bad place to set foot in when you arrive in Britain. And it's the perfect place to say goodbye.

One Perfect Day in London

On several occasions I have been asked what I would do in London if I only had a day to spend there. Usually, it's from a friend with a long layover. And it proves to be a very difficult question to answer. London always deserves more than a day. But what if you only had one day? I've traveled to London almost 20 times in the last fifteen years, and there are several things I do on every trip. And recently I was only there for a day. So, what would I do?

For the sake of this article, let's pretend that I'm already there and waking up in London.

First things first: Breakfast. If my hotel did not provide breakfast, I would venture out early, around 8 am, to find breakfast near my hotel. My current favorite place to stay in London is Hazlitt's in Soho, and we've discovered a great breakfast place called Balan's Soho Society Café, which has a wonderfully delicious breakfast.

After breakfast, I would walk through Chinatown, Leicester Square and make my way to Trafalgar Square. Not only is this my favorite public space in London but it's surrounded by great museums, most of which are free. I'd take a minute to say hello to Horatio Nelson, see if there is a new work of art on the Fourth Plinth, then I would make my next stop: The National Gallery. This is my favorite art gallery in London simply because of the breadth of the collection. There is something to see for every art interest. But I'm mostly interested in the Turners and Constables. So, I'll make my way to the room where they're kept (you may recognize the room from Skyfall). I'd stop and look at The Hay Wain, in fact, I would sit down and admire it for quite some time. This is probably the most famous landscape painting of Britain and sums up that romanticized view of rural England the British have. I'd also look at the Turners because I love Turner. As I only have one day, I would probably end my National Gallery sojourn here - unless there was a special exhibition worth seeing (always check!).

Normally, after this, I'd walked along the Thames down to the Palace of Westminster. But since Big Ben is covered in scaffolding until the 2020s, it's not a scene I need to see right now. Instead, I want to visit some bookstores.

I love bookstores in London. I love bookstores in general. But British bookstores are special in that you will find a completely different selection of books than you would find in an American bookstore. It's an Anglophile's dream. You can find Britain's bestsellers, and discover

British authors you may never have heard of in the USA. Now, it's very, very hard to pick a favorite bookstore here. But since I only have this one day, I'm going to pick Hatchards which is the oldest bookstore in London, dating back to 1797! I must spend at least an hour here. The best word to describe this bookstore is 'stately.' It's very much the type of store you would expect the aristocracy to buy their books at during the height of British Imperialism.

I would pay particular attention to the history and 'British' sections on the ground floor, then fan out and explore the rest of the store. My interests usually gravitate towards non-fiction more than fiction. Many newer books will be signed by the authors, as many big-name authors will make a stop at Hatchards when their books come out. Inevitably, I will end up with more books in my hands that I will be able to fit into my luggage home. That's where the personal service Hatchards offers come in handy. Depending on how many books you've bought (and how much you're willing to pay), they will gladly ship your books home for you. It's always a treat a few days after returning from London to receive a gift from yourself from Hatchards. I also recommend joining their email list so you can order books from them when you return home (they don't have an online store, you have to email or call to place an order).

By this point, after ogling some art and buying too many books, I will inevitably be ready to eat some lunch. There are unlimited options in London. But since I'm in London not far from several locations, I will opt for Nando's. Nando's is not British in any way, but it's one of the most popular restaurants in Britain. This South African/Portuguese fusion restaurant specializes in one thing: jerk chicken. Well two things, chicken and their delicious amazing chips (that's fries for my fellow Americans). The chicken is so good, and the chips are out of this world. Be warned; this chicken is SPICY hot (and you can get it hotter if you dare).

Now that I've eaten lunch, I've still got most of the day left. With that, I'll venture over to Covent Garden. Covent Garden is probably my second favorite place after Trafalgar Square. While it's easy to dismiss the place these days as just a fancy shopping mall and tourist trap, it's one of the most beautiful places in London that oozes in history. I've watched it change quite a bit over the years - I remember when there wasn't an Apple Store! - but I always come back. The actual old market building is a marvel of architecture, and I love browsing the artisans at the Apple Market, which lovingly attempts to reproduce Covent Garden's old market credentials (and don't miss the Jubilee Market as well!).

Oh, and if you're peckish after walking here after lunch - I would definitely stop and get a cookie at Ben's Cookies. It's not hyperbole to sit here and type that these are the most amazing cookies on the planet. They're incredible. Don't buy one, buy a box because they make a great snack in the hotel for the rest of your trip. After this, I'd walk over to Long Acre and find the Muji store. Muji is a Japanese brand that has stores all over Britain. They make the best stationery and pens and whenever I'm in London I stop in to restock. I also buy their orange soap. I've been doing it since my first visit to London. Their mandarin orange soap smells lovely, you can't get it in the USA, and whenever I smell the soap back home, it reminds me of London.

All right, I've done enough shopping. It's time for some more culture. At this point, I'd hop on the Tube. Riding the tube is a tourist attraction experience of its own. While it's not perfect and can get very hot in the summer, I just love the Tube. It's the quickest and cheapest way to get around central London other than walking. There's just something special about the smell of the Tube, and the feeling of the wind on your face as the train approaches you on the platform.

Where am I going? I'm taking the Tube to Westminster to visit the Churchill Cabinet War Rooms. Everyone who visits London must visit this place at least once. This is where Churchill led Britain to victory during World War II and understanding what a critical event this is in British history is vital for any understanding of modern Britain. It's also now home to a dedicated Churchill Museum so that you can get a picture of Churchill's entire life, not just the war years. Book ahead, this place can get quite crowded. It's not to be missed.

So, by this point, you're probably exhausted, and it's now dinner time. What better way to end your day than by having dinner at a London pub? Since you're in Westminster, why not go to The Two Chairmen? They have a great menu, and the pub is small and intimate. Best of all, it's popular with people who work in the British government, so you might find yourself rubbing shoulders with an MP or Cabinet Secretary.

After a leisurely pub dinner, I'm still not done with my one perfect day. There's still a whole evening ahead. And what better way than to spend it by going to a West End play? Skip the big-budget tourist trap musicals like Les Mis or Mamma Mia and instead see what's currently the 'hot play' in town. This is your chance to see famous British actors (and sometimes American as well) on the stage and in person. A few recent examples - Jeeves and Wooster (with Stephen Mangan), Travesties (with Tom Hollander), The Moderate Soprano (with Roger Allam) and King Lear (with Ian McKellan). Also, be sure to check what's currently on at the National Theatre and South Bank Centre. If there's not a play currently on you want to see, check St Martin in the Fields Church as they have evening music performances all year and it's a lot of fun listening to classical music in this beautiful old church.

After all of this, I will surely be ready for bed. My day in London may be over, but for me, it was perfect. I hope you can find your own perfect day in London and make the most of it. And if you only had that one day, I hope you can come back as soon as possible.

The Perfect Travel Partner

My wife is not an Anglophile. I don't hold it against her. Big of me, I know. If anything, she could be charitably described as a reluctant Anglophile. She loves me and understands how important England is to me, so comes along for the ride. And we've been on lots of rides together and she has grown to love Britain in her own way, but not nearly as much as me. It turns out, though, that despite her general disinterest in all things British, she's the perfect travel partner.

Our first adventure together was to London in 2004. We did not get off to an auspicious start and she was in tears by the end of the trip. Thankfully, it wasn't my fault. It was the fault of the British people. She could only handle so much coldness. I did not have the best experience on my first trip to London either. But when she and I went together in 2004, I was determined to love Britain now that I knew what to expect. What I discovered was that watching her discover the wonders of London for the first time, made me fall more in love with London and more in love with her.

On that first trip together, we took the Heathrow Express into London's Paddington Station. This is one of the most expensive ways to get into London. But we booked ahead and got a great deal. It's fast. It literally only takes 15 minutes, which is wonderful after you've just gotten off a seven-hour transatlantic flight. The train pulled into the station, we gathered our bags and exited the train (or alighted). I started traipsing along the platform, ready to get our London trip started. It took me a moment to realize that Jackie had paused and was standing there in awe.

"It's amazing," she said to me as I caught back up to her. "It's like right out of a storybook."

It was the best thing she could have said to me. The entire rest of the trip, I saw London with new eyes, her eyes and it was wonderful. Everything to her was amazing, interesting, beautiful. So, it became amazing and beautiful to me. As we sat for a hearty British breakfast in a small local café in Lancaster Gate, the sun was shining in through the window, and we had a wonderful view of a street of mews flats. It was magical. So were the chips (fries to my American readers). Yes, I had chips with breakfast. Because it's Britain and chips are an anytime food to me.

I ran the poor girl ragged, however. She learned a new phrase that trip: travel Jon-style.

And by the last day, despite us being only twenty years old, I'd exhausted her.

She was emotionally (we'd had a major life event - we got engaged) and physically exhausted (I didn't let her rest because I WANTED TO SEE EVERYTHING!).

So, it was only fair when we were in the airport, trying to go home and something didn't go right, or someone was particularly cold and rude, that she collapsed into a ball of tears.

"The British are just so COLD." She sobbed.

I did my best to comfort her (if she's reading this, she may think otherwise).

A few years later, we were both still in college, working menial jobs full time and then some. Christmas was always a struggle for us. But we always managed to have a wonderful Christmas together. I had no idea, really, what Jackie was going to get me for Christmas. So, it was with complete surprise that when I opened my large box, which she'd used to throw me off, I found a flag and a plane ticket inside to London.

She'd been listening to me moan for months about how much I missed England and how much I wanted to go back more than anything. But we couldn't afford to go - and couldn't afford to go together. So she saved and borrowed and managed to get enough money together to buy just me a plane ticket with the blessing to go by myself and make the most of London without her.

It was the purest act of love towards me she'd ever done for me up to that point. I simply could not believe it. She knew how bad I wanted to be there; she recognized how much it meant to me to go and then did everything she could to buy me a plane ticket to go. So, of course, I had to go.

As I excitedly began the trip planning process, of all the things I wanted to do, I became a bit sad, to be honest. They were all things I wanted to do with her. It felt wrong to go without her, wrong to see so many cool things and not take her. Wrong to not wake her up early, give her inadequate coffee and then run her ragged through London all day.

So I did the only sensible thing a few months later. I used a credit card that I should not have had, to buy her a ticket so she could come with me. It was one of the best decisions I ever made.

I've been to Britain without her since several times. Sometimes I go on business, and one of us has to stay home and keep up the home-front. Sometimes there's a major royal event, and she can't get away from her commitments. I don't like going without her. I love being in Britain, but when I'm there without Jackie it feels just a bit empty. Last year, I went to Britain twice without her - once to Prince Harry's wedding and the other to a rural writing retreat in the Lake District. By the time I was done in the Lake District, I was quite ready to be done exploring so many beautiful places without her. I just bloody missed my travel partner.

We've been on so many great adventures together. We found Gold Hill together. We got lost walking in the English countryside together. We laughed as we got stuck and fell into English mud together. We survived traveling to the Diamond Jubilee celebrations with our very young children together. We survived five weeks of Christmas holiday travel with our very young children. We found an abandoned village, explored grand stately homes, crossed miles of bridges, rode through the Chunnel. We drove from Land's End in Cornwall to John O'Groats in Scotland.

Ernest Hemingway once said, "Never go on trips with anyone you do not love." In my opinion, that is the only way to travel. Trips without Jackie feel like trips that shouldn't have happened. They feel like stolen time. What good is an amazing experience if she's not there to share it with me? When I was in the Lake District, I drove across the Hardnott Pass, the steepest and most dangerous road in Britain. Doing it by myself felt like a hollow victory. I would much rather have had her in my passenger seat, having an anxiety attack over the drop next to the rode or the steepness of the gradient and squealing whenever a passing car wanted to get by. Imagining her in my head during the drive just didn't do the trick.

That one time in college wasn't the only time she selflessly sent me off to England. A few years ago, I managed to snag tickets to a special tour of an abandoned Tube station, and since we had so much going on at home, she told me to just go. Buy a ticket, go for a long weekend and come home. So I bought the ticket, and that was the plan. Then a few weeks before the trip, I needed an emergency surgery. It was very unusual, and up till that point, I'd never had surgery for any reason. So it was a big deal, and it took it out of me.

I was laid up in bed for days, stressed as my trip to London was only a few weeks away. I had to heal quickly so I could go. I'd booked the cheapest ticket in Economy to make the trip affordable and planned to stay at a budget hotel. Jackie was determined to make sure I still went, so when the doctor gave the go-ahead, that it would be fine, I was very relieved. But Jackie knew that I could not be trusted by myself. I still needed to take it easy, I could not overdo it on the trip.

And the particular surgery I'd gotten made the prospect of sitting in

Coach for seven hours a bad idea.

So, for my own safety, we used the rest of our airmiles and managed to snag her a seat in Business class. Jackie was able to come along with me. And British Airways were very accommodating - they'd known about my surgery and managed to get my Economy ticket upgraded so that we could sit together in Business class in the 'King and Queen' seats. We had a very comfortable trip. I did not overdo it because Jackie simply would not let me. The abandoned Tube Station tour was amazing.

And my wife was amazing through it all.

I highly recommend everybody get a Jackie.

You won't regret it.

The Library of Dreams

Did you know that St Paul's Cathedral has a library? You probably didn't know because it's not something that is open to the public. In fact, it's in a part of the cathedral that is rarely open to the public - the Triforium. The Triforium is essentially St Paul's attic. It's where they keep the bits and bobs that aren't on public display; such as the scale wooden model that Sir Christopher Wren made to show the King his plan for his new cathedral. The model was amazing, but what I really fell in love with was the library.

We almost didn't see it - as the tour guide thought it was closed. But it was open. When the big wooden doors creaked open, we were treated to a room awash in late afternoon golden sunshine and the most marvelous old book smell. The tannin from hundreds of old leather books, carefully preserved across the centuries. A mixture of old leather, paper, and ink. If you could bottle the smell, it would make an excellent perfume for book nerds. The room is filled wall to wall with old books, with only a few dating back to before the cathedral was constructed. Many were donated as part of a massive collection.

Our little group was surprised to see there was a man in there, bespectacled as you would expect, behind a computer screen. He was both excited and alarmed to see people in his ecclesiastical sanctuary. It looked like we were interrupting his day, but he dutifully jumped up to give us an ad-hoc tour of this quiet and private domain. It was just us and the books. Artifacts from the cathedral's history were scattered across tables, in a seeming unorganized jumble. Busts and statues of the men who built the library or donated books to it look down from various aspects.

The library's original collection was mostly destroyed in the Great Fire of London in 1666. Wren's library chamber was restocked by the Commissioners for rebuilding St Paul's. They bought collections, including valuable Bibles and liturgical texts, and were fortunate to receive a generous bequest in 1712 of nearly 2,000 volumes from the library of Henry Compton, late Bishop of London. In 1783, the library of John Mangey, Vicar of Dunmow and Prebendary of St Paul's, was added. In the 19th century, extensive collections of ecclesiastical tracts and pamphlets were brought in.

The library is two stories high, with books stacked as high on old wooden shelves as they can be. Everything looks cataloged and organized; I suspect the life's work of several generations of librarians.

The scale of the place is a sight to behold, tucked away in the massive stone arches of the cathedral that Wren built. It's truly a remarkable place, filled with treasures beyond compare. The librarian talked to us about the books in the collection and how they care for them, ensuring that they survive the ravages of decay. I don't remember anything he said because I was in complete awe of the place.

I think about that library often. It is a place of dreams.

Parsnip Chips

We were somewhere in Hampshire. We were hungry. It was Sunday. Nothing was open. We had a two-year-old and a six-month-old baby with us in our hire car. We were tired from being in the car most of the day. We were far from any large towns with anything resembling fast food. Then it clicked with us, we could have Sunday Roast.

We just needed to find a pub offering Sunday Roast, and that would be perfect.

After a quick search on our phone, we found a nearby pub that sounded charming. The White Hart. Or White Swan. Or White King. I don't remember, it doesn't matter. We parked the car in the local library parking lot and walked in the rain to the pub. It looked a bit tired on the outside. The town was dead, as you would expect on a Sunday, but we were slightly concerned that we didn't see much activity around the pub itself.

That should have been the warning.

We went inside; it was warm and dry, which was welcoming. We found ourselves to be the only patrons. Clearly Sunday Roast was going on. But it wasn't clear which kind of pub it was - did we get table service? Did we order at the bar? Was the restaurant separate? We were too tired and wet with cranky kids to figure it out. After we settled in, a waitress appeared and explained the procedure.

It was a Sunday Roast CARVERY. We'd stumbled into a pub offering a buffet for Sunday Roast. I don't know about you, but we have a generally anti-buffet policy in this family—too many bad experiences. Still, we were already in there. It was warm and dry. We were hungry. We went with it anyway.

We took turns minding the kids while we went up to the carvery to pick our food. I opted for the beef. Roast potatoes are the traditional potato with Sunday roast, but I didn't want potatoes. I wanted chips. I scanned the buffet, and it looked like I saw chips. Jackpot! I got my beef, some sides and pointed at the chips and indicated I wanted those.

I sat down to tuck in. The beef was overcooked and flavor-less. But it was hot, and it was food. The veggies were fine. Then… I took a bite of one of my chips after dipping it in some ketchup. It was…. Crunchy. But I went with it. The flavor was really off. It tasted unlike any chip I've ever had. It was not what I was expecting. But I went with it, thinking maybe it was some kind of local culinary delicacy that fried them differently. I ate a whole one, and thought it rather odd it was taking so long to eat.

When I was done with the first one, I washed it down with my drink and ate some more meat. Then I decided to have another chip… I bit into it again.

"These chips taste funny," I mentioned to my wife, Jackie. Chewing one, and chewing it slower and slower, my mouth not wanting to have it inside anymore.

"Then don't eat them," she responded, thinking I meant funny as it would make me ill.

"No, here, try." I picked one up and handed it to her.

She bit into it and spit it out.

"That's not a chip," she said.

"What is it?"

"It's a parsnip. A fried parsnip."

"What the hell is a parsnip?"

"Not a chip, that's for sure."

I was suddenly put off my food. I thought I was eating chips, but instead something vile and awful and now my stomach was not happy that what was expected was not in it. We soon paid for our meal and left because both of us whispered that this was the worst meal we'd ever had in Britain. We pondered stopping at the convenience store on the way back to the car to get something to eat because we were still hungry.

To this day, I'm still unwilling to consider ever eating a parsnip.

Touching Concorde

I have seen and touched Concorde. Sadly, long after it was grounded. I became an adult just when they were making their final flights. Being able to afford to fly on one in my early 20s was an absurd pipe dream. I missed the supersonic age of air travel. One of Concorde's final destinations was Bristol Filton Airport, where every Concorde was built and had their first flights. It was only fitting that one of the final ones would go there. It's now marooned there.

The airport has been closed and redeveloped. It took over a decade for planners to finally build a museum around the Concorde; it sat outside for the intervening years. That new museum is now called Aerospace Bristol and it just recently opened. The museum is a guide to all the important flight developments that occurred at Bristol Filton, but by far the most important attraction is the new Concorde Hangar.

Set back from the rest of the museum in a separate building, a British Airways Concorde now sits properly in a dedicated hangar, with a multimedia experience all around it to educate visitors on the history of Concorde. Best of all you can walk around and under the Concorde and take in its immense size in person. What's striking is how HUGE Concorde is when you see it in person. But then how small it is on the inside when you see how cramped the seats were. There's a great video projected onto the side of the plane that gives a 10-minute history.

Upstairs, there's a small museum display that features various artifacts from Concorde's history. And then you're treated to being able to enter the plane itself. Previously one would have had to pay thousands of dollars to go onboard a Concorde; now anyone can for just a few pounds. It looks exactly as it did when they stopped flying. Unfortunately, you're not allowed to sit in the seats to get a real feel for what it would have been like to fly in the cramped interior.

If you're a fan of Concorde and aviation, a visit to this new museum is highly recommended. Looking around, though, you're hit with a realization. Once they brought Concorde into her new hangar, they sealed her in by building a wall. You get a huge feeling of sadness when you realize that there are no doors on this new hangar. Concorde is trapped inside and can never get out. She belongs in the air but will never experience it again.

Concorde died for lots of reasons but mostly because the airline industry doesn't have a vision beyond operating as cheaply as possible for passengers who want to pay as little as possible. The audio guide on the overhead speakers talked about how Concorde had revolutionized air travel, but really it didn't. The revolution died with Concorde's last flight in 2003. Supersonic air travel is dead. Concorde will now spend the rest of its existence in hangars like this, trapped, never going anywhere.

Old Stanfords

Stanfords is the first bookstore I visit on every trip to London. Stanfords is a bookstore that specializes solely in travel – guidebooks, travel writing, maps, etc. Sadly, they've recently moved from their Victorian building to a shiny new place down the road. And that's a shame.

Edward Stanford started the store in 1853 as a map seller, and the store expanded from there. It moved to its former location on Long Acre near Covent Garden in 1901. Its stately building was a joy to look at – let alone go inside. Every floor of the Victorian building was packed with maps, travel guides and inspirational travel writing; with beautiful hand-made globes and detailed atlases, as well as essential travel accessories for every occasion.

The ground floor featured best sellers and special offers, and you would often find non-travel related books that were currently popular. There was also a great section dedicated solely to London related books. There was often a special buy one, get one-half off, sale on the front tables – something I always took advantage of; one year I bought far too many books about British walks. Their British travel section was top notch, and you would find many lovely books about travel in the UK that you cannot find back home in the USA. My favorite section was the Ordnance Survey Map wall – they literally had every OS map that is printed and a handy guide on how to find the ones for the places you plan to go. OS maps are a must if you plan to do any walking in the English countryside.

The other floors were a dizzying array of travel books on every subject you can imagine. There's the section on travel writing. There's a section for pretty much every country in the world. If there is somewhere you want to go, Stanfords will have a book and map about it.

My favorite room was the map room.

Yes, it's a room just for buying maps.

You could find any kind of map you can possibly think of. Need a map for an expedition to the Himalayas? They have you covered. Need a map of the Shetland Islands? They have you covered. Need a map of your home state in America, they'll have that too. They have pretty much every map that's in print - and can print you a custom map if they don't have it. The printer sits there in the store, waiting to print the map of your dreams. It's incredible.

They had every travel book that's currently in print - and quite a few that are out of print too. No matter where you want to go in the world, they had a book for that. And if you cannot find the book, the knowledgeable staff will help you find it. Only have a vague idea of something you want to explore? Talk to the staff, they'll have suggestions and will know the perfect book. Don't want a guidebook but would rather read the latest travel tome from the likes of Bill Bryson or Paul Theroux? They'll have that too.

The hardest part is keeping your purchases to a reasonable amount to fit in your luggage for the return trip. I'm happy to report you don't need to worry about this. Stanfords will be happy to ship your purchase back home for you, for a reasonable price. Then a week from now, when you're back home and missing London, your order will arrive from Stanfords as a gift from your past self.

If you have any kind of travel dreams, Stanfords - even in its new location - is a place you must visit.

The Tradition Before Going to England

We all develop habits and traditions when we travel. Rituals. Rites of passage that help make the insanity of travel saner. The trip can't start properly until you do them. For the first few years of our travel to Britain, in the early 2000s, one of the unexpected traditions we started was to stop at a greasy old fast food restaurant on our way to the airport. It was called The Lure. The food was classic greasy fast food but with the best milkshakes on the planet.

I grew up eating at this place mostly because it was the closest fast-food restaurant to our house in Indiana. It used to be a prominent local chain, with several locations in the area but, in my late teens and early 20s, it was just down to the last holdout. The food was reliably tasty, but nothing special. What was special was the milkshakes, which most locals would agree were the best you could get anywhere around. No one knew why.

The drive-through always had a line around the building and out to the street. And the food was not fast; you had to sit and wait for them to make it fresh for you, a charming anachronism in a country that prides itself on instant food. If the line was long, you expected to sit and wait for it. It was always worth the wait. These were the days before smartphones, so when you waited you had to sit and ponder the world because there was nothing else to do. It was charming in its old-fashioned way - orange tiles on the floor, they only took cash.

As we left for our first trip to Britain together in 2004, Jackie and I found ourselves a bit hungry. So we decided to stop at The Lure on our way to the airport. It turned out to be the perfect pre-flight meal to fuel us up for the long drive to O'Hare and getting through Security. We liked it so much that the next year, on our next trip, we stopped there again on our way to the airport.

After that, it was just expected that we would stop at The Lure on our way to Britain. The trips could not start properly without our Lure burgers and milkshakes.

Then we moved away for a bit and weren't able to travel for a few years. So the tradition stopped, and we were hours away from The Lure. Then one day when we were passing by we saw that it was closed. A sign said it was temporary. We hoped it was.

It was not. Time moved on, and The Lure was closed forever. We miss it, even 15 years later, when we head to the airport to go to Britain. Now we just eat at the airport. But it's just not the same.

An Ode to Chunky Chips

My favorite British food is not what one would think. It's not a meat pie. It's not fried fish. It's not roast. It's not marmalade on toast. It's not lemon cake. I do love all of those things (well, except for the fish). No, my favorite British food is what we call fries - chips.

But not just any chips. Because there are many different kinds of chips in Britain.

No, I'm talking about chunky chips.

How does one describe a chunky chip? It's a bit like a steak fry, but much thicker. It has a more cubical shape and is usually much shorter. A 'proper' chip is usually made from Jersey potatoes; the best potatoes come from the Channel Islands. They're thick. They're usually double or tripled fried (meaning they're cooked more than once). They are not fried in oil. They are fried in beef dripping.

Your 'chip' mileage in Britain will vary greatly. But when you find the right chips, note the place down so you know you can return. They're usually golden brown on the outside. When you bite into them, they're perfectly fluffy and delicious. Perfect to be dipped in either vinegar or ketchup (I know this is sacrilege, but I like ketchup on my chips so deal with it, OK?). While chips are not traditionally part of Sunday Roast, I always get chunky chips to go with my roast. It's the best combination of beef and potatoes.

Sometimes, the best chips you'll get will be from the local greasy chipper. It will not be a chain. It will look rather grungy and dour on the outside. But when you go in and smell the fish, chicken and chips, you'll know you're at home. You're in the place of proper chips. I have never had proper chunky chips outside Britain. Most places in the USA that try fish and chips do both wrong. They give you fish strips instead of a massive slab of cod. They give you thin fries or steak fries instead of chunky chips.

When I peruse the local British ex-pat message board, chunky chips are always at the top of the list of things they miss about home. My local British food store even manages to stock frozen chunky chips that you can bake at home (BAKE! Are you insane?). But you can't get them here simply because the potatoes are all wrong. You need British or Channel Island potatoes. Proper potatoes. Fried in beef dropping, preferably three times.

Now, excuse me while I book a flight to Britain, just so I can have some chunky chips!

My Favorite Place in London

Trafalgar Square is my favorite place in London.

When looking back at all the trips we've taken over the years, there's one place we return to more often than others. And it's what is essentially London's front porch. After the area was pedestrianized in the early 2000s, Trafalgar Square became a center of celebrations (and protests) in London. It's where London's Christmas tree goes. It's where people go to celebrate a big event.

But more than that, I love the square itself. I'm a history enthusiast, and I greatly respect Horatio Nelson – the man at the top of the column in the center of the square. He represents the best of British historical figures. If I was making a ranking, I would place him after Churchill in British historical importance. He certainly was not a perfect man, but most historical figures are not perfect. They're human. It's fitting that the square is named after and is a tribute to his most important achievement, defeating the French at the Battle of Trafalgar.

Even the name Trafalgar evokes a certain amount of gravitas. It's not even an English place name, but it has become one thanks to the quirks of history. Nelson stands at the top of his monument – and it's really cool that it's the 'final' Nelson – blind in one eye and missing an arm – they did not sugarcoat him – gazing directly at the Houses of Parliament and towards the sea, his true home.

It's not just what's in the square or what it means historically; there are several things around the square that have played an important role in my 'London' travel life. Perched behind Nelson is, of course, The National Gallery, one of the finest art museums in the world, home to some of the most famous works of art ever created. But I particularly love that it's home to Britain's most famous and loved paintings like The Hay Wain by John Constable and the landscapes of JMW Turner. And it's all free to the public. You can walk in whenever it's open, and go look at your favorite painting completely for free, and crucially without a line to wait in. My local art museum, The Art Institute of Chicago, charges exorbitant admission fees to get in, so I can only go admire the great works there when money allows. When I'm in London, I can go look at world-class art, whenever I want, completely for free.

Then there's St Martin in the Field's Church across the way from the National Gallery. This beautiful old Neoclassical church is a feast for the eyes. But it's also home to a world-class music program, and one of the best things you can do if you're in London is to take in a musical performance in the church. The acoustics are wonderful, and Jackie and I have been on some of our best nights out in this church.

Trafalgar Square is a great place to pass through on your way to somewhere else in London. Get a sandwich from a nearby takeaway and have a seat and watch London go by. See the tourists from all over the world, enjoying the most beautiful spot in London. Watch London live its life as it passes through the square on its way to other places. And when Big Ben returns to service, enjoy looking at it and listening to its chimes.

The Concorde Room
and Piers Morgan

It was a trip of dreams. We'd been flown to Britain for free as a prize in a contest. On the way home, we would get to fly British Airways First Class, in a Queen of the Sky - a Boeing 747. It was a very unlikely thing to happen, for a couple in their late-20s running a new-fangled thing called a 'blog' that was taking the Anglophile world by storm. We couldn't believe our luck.

Everything about the experience was new to us and completely out of any frame of reference we ever had. For example, we didn't know that First Class passengers had their very own, exclusive lounge at Heathrow, separate from the 'regular' Business Class lounge. Suitably called the Concorde Room, this is where First Class passengers go to get pampered before getting on their long-haul flight where they also get... pampered.

It was a remarkable place. It was practically empty - there aren't many First Class passengers, after all. The staff to passenger ratio is stacked in the passenger's favor. There were so many people in the room, falling all over themselves to help us. I could get quite used to that.

The most surprising thing was that there was a restaurant in there, where you can eat for free before your flight. And a bar where you can drink for free. Or get a massage for free. Or read free newspapers. Everything is free. Though I supposed none of it was really free when you pay $12,000 for a ticket. We did not pay for our tickets; we were guests of the airline, so everything really was free for us. We couldn't believe our luck.

We sat down in the restaurant to eat. The menu was what I would describe as 'fancy.' But there was a burger. Service was attentive. The food was delicious.

Then a family, with all their luggage in tow, sat down next to us.

I didn't take much notice.

But my wife, Jackie, did.

"Jon," she whispered. "Is that... Piers Morgan?"

I looked over, and sure enough, it was indeed the feared presenter of America and Britain's Got Talent (this was long before his CNN days, he was still endearing to Americans at this time!).

"Oh my god, it is!" I tried to contain my excitement.

We listened intently as he and his family ordered breakfast. And they ordered something that wasn't on the menu.

I didn't know you could do that!

Well, Piers Morgan can.

He had scrambled eggs.

That sounded quite good.

We were fully and truly starstruck even though it was someone that we didn't necessarily worship. But we could get used to this kind of life, eating lunch next to the host of a major TV show.

I have nothing bad to say about the man. He was perfectly nice and respectful to the staff in the lounge. He chatted with his family. He ignored us. It's OK, I would ignore us too.

And that was my first brush with celebrity.

We finished our lunch, and before we knew it, boarded our plane home to Chicago (via Boston). The flight in the First Class cabin was glorious in every way. They served us steak! At 30,000 feet! Jackie fell ill (she was pregnant at the time with our son) and they took extra good care of her when she told them she was pregnant. We were treated exceptionally well for two people that clearly didn't belong in First Class (I was in a bloody t-shirt!).

Hopefully one day we can do it again and maybe run into our friend Piers Morgan (though nowadays he's known as being Britain's Top Bell-End… so maybe not).

Shake Shack after the Theater

One thing they don't tell you about plays is that they can be rather long affairs. Most plays will have an intermission and, before you know it, you've spent 4 hours in a theater for one show. Being used to 2-hour movies, you end up with the weird situation where you ate many hours ago, so by the time you leave the theater, late at night in London, you're starving again.

This happened to us a few years ago when we decided to treat ourselves to the hot play in town on our last night in London. It was a play that was generally sold out - but our hotel concierge managed to get us tickets. The play was the revival of Tom Stoppard's Travesties, a comedic play about a British envoy in 1917's Europe. The play centers on the figure of Henry Carr, an elderly man who reminisces about Zürich in 1917 during the First World War, and his interactions with James Joyce when he was writing Ulysses, Tristan Tzara during the rise of the Dada movement and Vladimir Lenin leading up to the Russian Revolution, all of whom were living in Zürich at that time.

Sounds dense, right?

It was. Frankly, I'd never heard of the play. We only wanted to go because the star of the show was Tom Hollander, a British actor whom we like quite a lot. I'm happy to report that the play was marvelous and Hollander was phenomenal.

But when we got out of the play, well past 11 pm, we were starving.

The theater was not far from our hotel, so we decided to just walk through Soho on the way back. Our tummies were rumbling.

We came upon the newly opened Shake Shack.

Now, at the time, Shake Shack was the hot new thing in America, and we had just gotten one in Chicago, but we'd never been. We were quite sick of all the different ways places in America make a hamburger. How could it be any different? Well, the smells coming out were nice, and it wasn't crowded, and it looked brightly lit.

So, despite never having been to a Shake Shack, we decided to give it a go - 4,000 miles from where Shake Shack was native.

Both tired from a long day in London, and hungry despite already having had dinner, the burger and fries presented by Shake Shack were the perfect after theater treat. The burgers were great, Jackie fell in love with them. And the milkshakes! They were divine. It was the perfect post-show antidote and helped us walk contentedly into the night back to our swank London hotel.

This was many years ago, and every time since when we've done a play in London, we have a new tradition, we make a point of stopping at a Shake Snack. Until last year, we still hadn't been to one in the USA! How funny, to fall in love with an American burger chain in a completely different country.

Snowdrops

I live in the mid-western United States. Every winter is pretty much the same. One thing happens every year that always makes winter a depressing prospect. Everything dies here in the winter.

The grass goes into hibernation and turns brown. The trees lose their leaves. All the greenery that is abundant in the spring, summer, and fall just disappears. If you're lucky, it'll be covered in a white coat of snow, which has a stark beauty all its own. If it's like any other winter, there won't be snow most of the time, and everything will be a dead muddy mess instead.

I've written many times before about my surprise that England in the dead of winter is still remarkably green. It's one of the things I love about the place so much - and why I'll always jump at the chance to visit England in the winter.

But it isn't just the grass that stays green.

They get blooming flowers in the winter!

I'm talking about snowdrops.

These remarkable little flowers carpet the English countryside, almost like a weed. They're everywhere. They're a small flower, whose key feature is a little white bell that hangs from the stalk. They grow in patches.

I first noticed them when we were on a walk through the Stourhead Gardens in January. It was such a novelty to me, to see a flower blooming in such large quantities in the dead of winter.

We're all familiar with the beauty of an English wood with a lovely carpet of bluebells in the English spring. But I would counter that you haven't seen anything until you've seen a snowdrop wood. Imagine instead a wood carpeted in beautiful white flowers, as far as you can see.

Some places, like Shaftesbury in Dorset, now have an annual snowdrop festival, where they celebrate this winter marvel. A harbinger of spring. A sign of the beauty of things to come. Something that brings a small bit of life and color to a dreary winter.

Snowdrops are marvelous little things. Be sure to stop and visit them if you happen to find yourself in England in the winter.

The Morning Walk in Shaftesbury

I always rise early in England. Every moment in England is precious, I don't like to waste more of it sleeping than I need to. Jackie likes to sleep in late, which is fine. So that means that this quiet time in the morning is for me and me alone. It's my chance to commune and connect with England in solitude.

When I'm in Shaftesbury I always try to do a quick morning walk. Nothing long or anything, just enough to wander around the town, see the views, explore the empty streets and usually pick up a newspaper or pastry from the local bakery.

Since we're usually there in the spring or winter, I always bundle up. More often than not, it's a bit wet. The sun rises a bit late in the winter months in England, so even around 8 am, the sun is still struggling to get over the horizon. Combine that with the cloudiness and the wet and you have a particular kind of fogginess that leads to the imagination wandering.

One expects a dragon to fly out of the clouds at any moment.

I always walk up Gold Hill, which is steep, so it's a bracing walk after you've just woken up. It helps with the waking up process! I'll usually walk up to the High Street, stopping to admire the view of Gold Hill and the Blackmore Vale (if you can actually see it!). Then I'll turn left, walk past the Oxfam Bookshop, and head onto the Park Walk, which is a lovely promenade that has a park and viewing area of the valley.

If I can't see anything, I won't linger, but if the way is clear, I'll stop and stay awhile, enjoying the green and pleasing view of the sun slowly bathing the vale in golden winter sunlight. I'll close my eyes and listen. Shaftesbury is a very quiet and still place, especially in the winter. Often the only sound will be the winter birdsong. Owls. Crows. Starlings. Pigeons. Larks. Doves. Blue tits. It's a symphony of sound that I can't hear anywhere else.

It is really and truly my happy place.

Depending on how I feel that morning, I'll walk further along the walk and into the local woods and then loop back to the High Street. If I'm feeling really ambitious, I'll walk to the other side of the town and look at the views going south. If it's clear, you can see King Alfred's Tower at Stourhead.

If we hadn't already, I'll stop at the greengrocer and get some fresh fruit for the day - a banana is a critical fuel for the traveler in England. Then I'll pop into the newsagent and pick up the day's newspaper. Always

The Times. I'm in for a particular treat if it's Sunday - as the Sunday papers are a marvel of reading - it will take you all day to read through them properly. If I haven't already, I'll probably pick up the latest issue of Country Life and Dorset Life, two of my favorite magazines.

By this point, it's getting late in the morning, and I'm probably getting hungry. So I'll walk back towards the High Street and stop at the bakery. I'll pick up some breakfast pastries - usually a muffin or a donut—something for Jackie when she wakes up. Arms full with newspapers and pastries, I'll head back towards the Town Hall, walk around it and then find myself back at Gold Hill. If it's started to clear, I'll stop briefly and admire the view. Then make my way gingerly down the cobbles, carrying my provisions.

I'll unlock the front door of the cottage, walk in, then close it behind me. The walk is over, the English morning is over.

But a whole day ahead in England awaits. What a way to start it!

The Pub After the Royal Wedding

I was tired, hot, sweaty, and starving. I'd just experienced a Royal Wedding with my own eyes. I'd stood on The Mall for almost 8 hours, listening to the wedding ceremonies of William & Kate. My whole body ached and I was hot. Thankfully, a shower back at the hotel cooled me a bit and helped with the smell! Good thing this book doesn't have smell-o-vision! It was mid-afternoon by this point. The high of the wedding had run its course. Now I was just hungry and tired. I hadn't had lunch because I was busy covering the wedding, and my snacks had run out hours before.

So I did what any sensible Brit would do after a major occasion. I went down the pub (this is a British phrase, it's not grammatically incorrect!).

There was a nice pub right across from my hotel in St James. I don't remember the name of it. It doesn't really matter. It was English. It was 'pubby.' They had food. I met up with the colleague who was with me covering the wedding, who was also exhausted and hungry. And as we made ourselves comfortable after ordering the food, the most remarkable thing happened.

The BBC replay of the Royal Wedding was starting on the TVs lining the pub walls. Now, while I got to experience the wedding while covering it, I didn't actually see most of what people saw on TV, I only heard it over the loudspeakers set up outside Buckingham Palace. So this tired Anglophile was delighted to be able to sit and watch the highlights reel the BBC was kindly replaying for everyone.

The pub was packed with tired and sweaty Brits who'd also been on the Mall that day, and it became completely silent. You could hear a pin drop as everyone sat with rapt attention, watching the proceedings all over again. Food appeared in front of us - good hearty pub grub. I believe I had a burger and chunky chips. My colleague had bangers & mash.

And we sat and ate and drank and watched the proceedings all over again. It was a truly magical moment. I got to live through the Royal Wedding as a communal experience for a second time, while the high of a successful day wore off. I got to see what the rest of the world saw while I was working to cover it.

After it was over, I rolled myself back to the hotel room for a rest in bed, watching more telly. And what came on right after the wedding replay ended? None other than Wallace and Gromit.

I can't think of a better way to end a perfectly British day, such as a Royal Wedding.

Finding Peak Happiness Through the Hardknott Pass

I was sitting in a hay barn at the end of a hot July day in the Lake District. Outside the door was a view of the beautiful Matterdale Valley. Inside was a group of writers, all on a high after having finished an intensive writers' workshop. Sitting across from me was a best-selling author. All of us were exhausted, enjoying final cups of tea while we said our goodbyes. After having been around the famous writer for a few days, feeling starstruck had begun to wear off. And I was brave enough to ask a question.

"If you had one day left in the Lake District," I began, "what would you tell someone to do before they left?"

He was taken aback by the question.

"Not something you ever really think about living here, because you're a local," he responded. Then he began to think.

After a moment's pause, he said, "I would visit the Hardknott Roman Fort. It's perfectly situated with incredible views, and it's a historical and magical place. And you get the bonus of driving through the Hardknott Pass."

"Then that's what I'm going to do," I said confidently.

As a travel writer, I've heard of the Hardknott Pass. I'm also well aware that I should be terrified of it. It is one of the steepest roads in Britain, sporting a 30% gradient. Not only that, its course is mostly a single-track lane with precipitous drops along the edges. It is not a road for the faint of heart.

Over a decade ago, Anglotopia had a columnist, Lisa Coulson, who lives in Northern England, and she attempted to drive the Hardknott Pass. She did it in a manual car. Doing the Pass in a manual is a rite of passage in driving in Britain simply because shifting gears on the steep gradients is such a challenge. By the time she'd made it over the Pass she was in tears and described it as one of the scariest experiences of her life.

The Hardknott Pass is one of the oldest routes in Britain; it was originally laid out by the Romans. Though they preferred their roads to be straight, there is nothing straight about the Hardknott Pass.

The Pass is just over a mile in length, but it will take you quite some time to get through it. When you look at the Pass on a two-dimensional map, it's lying to you. It looks like a relatively straight line — no big deal. The map is very wrong. If the map was in three dimensions, you would see how steep it really is. You need to look at the Ordnance Survey

map to get an idea of how steep the Pass is.

The name itself has such a romantic sound to it. The name Hardknott took some linguistic digging. On the surface, it sounds like what it says on the tin - a hard place. It comes from the old Norse 'haror' meaning a rather difficult and inaccessible place. The 'knott' part of the name has two suspected origins – 'knutr' meaning knot in Old Norse or 'knut,' meaning peak in Norwegian. The name literally means a difficult pass over a peak. The name is not Roman in origin, obviously, that came later. The Romans called this place 'Mediobogdum.'

While there has always been a route through these valleys, the paved road itself is a relatively recent creation. In fact, there was much opposition to the creation of a road through the Hardknott Pass. According to The Times of London, in 1934 a public consultation was held on the construction of roads in the Lake District and one local vicar argued that there shouldn't even be a road over the Hardknott Pass: "He suggested that the Lake District, because of its small area, unlike Scotland or Norway, was unsuitable for cutting up by Trunk Roads, which would destroy its remoteness, still part of its charm."

I'm happy to report, Canon Wilcox, Vicar of Kirkoswald, that you were wrong and the Lake District still retains its remoteness. I barely encountered any people on my journey through the Hardknott Pass. Though it's apparent that the Lake District landscape has now developed almost entirely to accommodate leisure in all its forms it should be said it is still very much a working landscape - especially for farmers.

It has always been on my 'Britain Bucket List' to journey through the Hardknott Pass, and this seemed as good a time as any. It's not every day that you get a personal recommendation from a best-selling author.

On my final day in the Lake District, I woke up and had breakfast as early as possible. I wanted to have as much time as possible for my quest, and I wanted to get going before the roads got too crowded with my fellow tourists. My car was a Toyota Hybrid (not a Prius, a hatchback of some kind, sorry I don't know my cars very well). I didn't choose this car, it's the one I ended up with in the Hertz rental lottery. I did not like the car. It did not have the comforting sound of most diesel British cars. In fact, it was silent most of the time. But it did have one advantage for my journey that day, it had an automatic transmission.

In theory, going over the Hardknott pass won't be as challenging without having to think about shifting the gears. In theory.

I set my route on my phone and mounted it on the dashboard. I was a good hour drive away from the start of the Pass so, for the next hour, I would get the sublime pleasure of driving through the Cumbrian

countryside on a sunny summer morning. The sky was clear and deep blue, with barely a wisp of clouds. Perfect for a morning drive. I tuned my radio to ClassicFM and began the drive.

My initial route took me south down the A591 and along Thirlmere and then along Grasmere. This was the Lake District at its most resplendent. It's such an interesting landscape to drive through, and I almost wish I'd been a passenger so I could fully appreciate all its variety. When driving on the curvy roads, at 50 miles an hour, one must be exceptionally mindful. After all, I didn't buy the extra car insurance when I rented... (I live on the edge).

I passed through Grasmere, which I hadn't been able to visit on my trip. I didn't have time to stop, and it was too early for anything worth seeing to be open. Don't worry; I intend to return simply because Grasmere is beautiful. It is a lovely Lake District village. It's also home to the finest bookstore in the Lake District (Sam Read Booksellers) and Dove Cottage, the home of William Wordsworth.

After passing through Grasmere, my satnav guided me to the roads to the west of the lake. From this point on it would be single-track lanes all the way through the Pass. As I drove along Grasmere, I encountered many walkers and cyclists going about their mornings. The opportunities for walking around the Lake District are practically infinite. It felt rather odd to be experiencing this landscape from inside a comfortable air-conditioned car.

At this point, I began climbing. The car didn't struggle, but I occasionally had to apply more gas than I would expect to in a normal car. Such is the experience of driving a hybrid. The thing loved it when I went downhill as the breaks recharged the batteries. But with so much climbing and the distances involved, it wouldn't really use the batteries. And it really confused the computers that control the car. It would only get more confused as my day went on.

In addition to dodging hill walkers, I also had to dodge sheep, which ply the hills of the Lake District and the roads as well. It's part and parcel of travelling through a working landscape like the Lake District, you just have to be mindful of sheep as well as walkers. While it's easy to be annoyed when you have to stop for a bunch of sheep to pass, it gives you a moment to enjoy the landscape. The roads are very narrow up there, usually buttressed on both sides by moss-covered ancient dry-stone walls. Barely enough room for two cars to pass each other, which means there is lots of reversing to get to a spot to let oncoming traffic pass.

The further I climbed the more traffic thinned out. It was beginning to feel like I was alone in the world in my quest to climb one of the steepest roads in Britain. The car climbed and climbed. The landscape was green and lush, all the trees were in full bloom. I'm sure the Lake District is beautiful year-round, even in the harsh winters up there, but it has to be at its most beautiful in the summer when it's completely alive. Being there makes me feel alive.

Even with terrible hay fever which, thankfully, being sealed in the car meant I was getting relief from.

And then there was a turn, but this one was special. This turn had a warning.

It warned me of the 30% gradient and that the road required "Extreme Caution. Narrow route, severe bend, winter conditions can be dangerous. Unsuitable for caravans. Please drive slowly." This must be it, I was unceremoniously entering the Hardknott Pass. The road was immediately steeper.

I had that nervous feeling in my stomach. I was confident I could do the drive, but I was very excited to be doing it. At first, it didn't seem so bad.

The climb became more intense and the road narrowed, making encountering oncoming traffic rather more nerve-wracking. The landscape began to open up, and you could clearly see the fells all around. They were bare, treeless, and harsh. Cottages and farms became fewer and fewer. Very few people live up here and those that do take a particular form of bravery as they can be completely cut off in the winter.

But not on a sunny day in July.

I crossed a cattle grid, and there was another warning sign, the gradient was going to get much steeper (at this point I'm wondering how much bloody steeper!). The road actually flattened out for a bit as I went through a valley, and I wondered if that was it.

Then I began to climb again, past an abandoned farmstead. The car began to struggle as I had to apply more gas on the pedal. And then all of a sudden it got incredibly steep. And I climbed. And climbed. And climbed. The climb got so steep that I couldn't see over the humps for oncoming traffic. So I had to take it slow. Knowing British roads, a car could magically appear at any time around any blind corner or bump.

Ahead I could see the road snaking over the hills. It was going to get steeper.

And then the dry-stone wall stopped, and all that was between me and a precipitous drop down a mountain valley was a small hump of grass. At this point, I could only go forward and hug the right side of the road, ever mindful I could encounter an approaching car at any second and have to veer over, hopefully not into the valley below!

Despite the fear, and more signs warning me of more steep gradients, I was in awe. It was an incredibly beautiful landscape, and the downside

Road suitable for cars and light vehicles only

Unsuitable for all vehicles in winter conditions

30%

Narrow route severe bends

of being such a focused driver was that I couldn't pause to enjoy it. There were occasional pull-offs to let an oncoming car come that allowed me to stop and enjoy the scenery. It was incredible. And I'm going to do the unwriterly thing and just apologize that I'm going to run out of adjectives to use here.

I let a farm truck pass and then it was just me, the road and a few sheep and I continued to climb.

I climbed more. The hybrid motor was not pleased with me. Then I found a stop off and took some pictures and looked at what I'd just driven through. It was a completely different perspective, and it was incredible to think I'd just driven through that! And not messed my drawers!

After a final climb, I began to descend into the valley beyond. I'd done it. I'd gone through the Hardknott Pass. Now, where was the fort?

I drove on and descended more.

And then I came to the base of another valley and then a turn off with more warnings. Wait a second.

The sign said Hardknott Pass.

I literally exclaimed for no one to hear, "That wasn't it!"

A quick look at the map showed I'd just gone through the Wrynose Pass, which comes before the Hardknott Pass. I'd just done the most challenging and most beautiful drive in my life, and it wasn't even the right one!

As I entered the actual Hardknott Pass, the signs took on a more sinister warning, which made sense. I can only imagine being up here in the winter and unable to pass through. It would be terrifying and dangerous.

I began to climb again. This time it was steeper. The landscape was barren. I'd only passed one lonely cottage on the way. There were only Herdwick sheep, who wandered in the road like they owned the place, which of course they did. The hills were surprisingly bare of trees. Despite the barren feel, it was green all around except where the grass could not grow.

The etiquette on driving this route is that you're supposed to get out of the way of oncoming traffic coming through the western approach of the Pass. And I dutifully did this whenever I encountered a car. Everyone was very courteous. I always got a wave of thanks when I pulled aside or reversed to let someone pass.

And now the steep gradients really began. The road twisted and turned and climbed all within a few feet of each other. There were no stone walls — just grass verges. Thankfully, so far there weren't any steep drops along the side like through the Wrynose Pass. The car really struggled up the very steep climb. The turns were sharp, you couldn't see much beyond them. So you had to take it slowly. I can only imagine how terrible this would be in a manual. The car was doing OK, though it didn't like climbing, the transmission kept up. My breathing deepened. I was exceptionally nervous about being on such an incline. I'd been on inclines before driving through the Appalachian Mountains, but nothing this steep before.

There were spots on bends where the road would widen, allowing you to pull off and then see if anything was approaching. This was very helpful. There were also places you could pull off in an emergency.

And then with one final climb, I was up and over the Pass. Off in the distance, I could see the Irish Sea. And the road began to descend quickly. Instead of climbing a steep incline, I would descend down a steep incline. I would have to do it just as slowly and carefully. I came across a lady doing the climb in a low-profile BMW, and she kept getting stuck and bottoming out trying to make the sharp turns.

The Esk Valley spreads out before you and it is, for lack of a better word, breathtaking. Going over the Hardknott Pass, for me, was peak happiness. Nothing could have ruined the moment. Well, maybe a car accident!

Soon I could see the Hardknott Roman Fort ruins and kept them in my sights as I approached. And now the reward for enduring such a challenging drive. I pulled off into a car park, gathered my gear and began to explore the Roman ruins. As you climb into the ruins, you can immediately see why the Romans built a fort there. It was ideally situated to monitor the Hardknott Pass but also to keep an eye on the sea beyond for enemy ships.

What struck me most of all was the wind. The wind through the valley was continuous, thanks to the wind tunnel effect of the shape of the valley. The second thing you notice is the sheep. They are everywhere, and it is a symphony of sheep bleating. It's quite something to have a Roman ruin all to yourself, with just a few sheep for company. I took my time exploring the various locations of the installation, dodging sheep poo. It was massive.

It was no small outpost of the Roman Empire; this was a true stamp of Roman civilization on the harsh Northern English landscape. Not much is left save for the few stone outlines of buildings, some of which have been built back up with recent excavations and restorations. But the fort itself was long ago looted for its stone, which you can find in the buildings of the surrounding valleys.

It's easy to imagine yourself as a Roman soldier, standing on this spot, probably thinking it was godforsaken with an unceasing wind. In the distance, you can see the Irish Sea. This was literally the western

edge of the known Roman world.

The fort was built between about 120AD and 138AD and was abandoned during the Antonine advance north into Scotland during the mid-2nd century. The fort was then reoccupied around 200AD and continued in use until the last years of the 4th century when the Romans abandoned Britain altogether. It's been a ruin ever since. The National Trust now owns the land it sits on, and English Heritage maintains the fort itself. Though, I'm sorry to report, not maintained very well. Most of the signage is falling apart, and it's difficult to tell what is what. It was a beautiful and magical place to visit.

As I walked back to my car, I looked back towards the Hardknott Pass and was chuffed that I'd actually managed to do it and chuckled a bit at the sight of other cars slowly making their way down the road. I'd achieved something I've wanted to do for years. It was a challenge. It was beautiful. And I certainly wasn't going back that way. No, my journey would continue on through the Esk Valley to a steam railway and Muncaster Castle, where I would take a much easier but circuitous route along the coast and through Windermere back to my hotel for my final night in Cumbria.

ABOUT THE AUTHOR

Jonathan Thomas was born in the early 80s, and apart from a short stint in Texas, spent most of his childhood in Northern Indiana, just outside of Chicago. During high school, he found a poster of Gold Hill, in Shaftesbury, Dorset in a Hobby Lobby and instantly fell in love. That poster hung on his wall for years and motivated him to visit England for the first time in 2001 and finally to visit Shaftesbury in 2004. It was a life-changing experience for him.

Jonathan met his wife Jacqueline in remedial math class at Columbia College in Chicago. Both later attended Purdue University, where they completed their studies. Jonathan studied English literature and language. During their college years, they took their extra student aid money and financed yearly trips to England where they gained their first travel knowledge and eventually cemented their mutual love for all things British (well, Jonathan's anyway).

After college, Jonathan went to work in the internet marketing world, changing jobs every few years as he gained experience in digital marketing. He could not find a website that fed his Anglophilia, so he decided to start one. In 2007, in a closet in Chicago, he founded Anglotopia.net as a home online for Anglophiles around the world. It rode the blogging wave of the late 2000s and became the world's most trafficked website dedicated to all things British.

Anglotopia became Jonathan's full-time job in 2011, weeks before the Royal Wedding of William and Kate. Over the years, he's attended other major Royal events, appeared on the BBC and other media venues, and has been published in The Art of Manliness, The Independent and Dorset Life magazine. He publishes articles every day on Anglotopia.net and its sister website Londontopia.net, and puts out a quarterly print magazine.

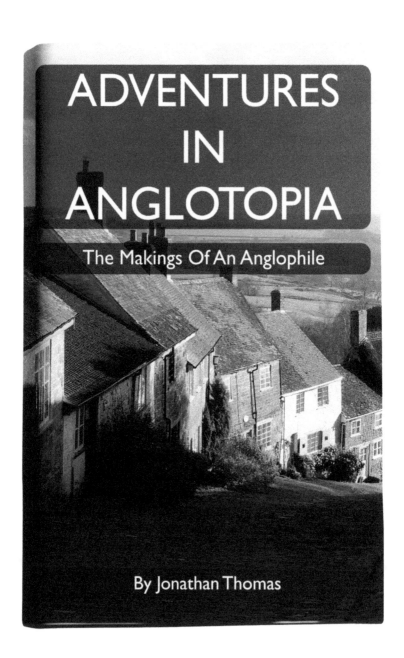

ADVENTURES IN ANGLOTOPIA

The Makings Of An Anglophile

By Jonathan Thomas

Now Available from Booksellers Everywhere

Adventures in Anglotopia
The Makings Of An Anglophile

By Jonathan Thomas

What makes an Anglophile? What makes someone love a country not their own? Adventures in Anglotopia is a journey to answer this question, framed through a childhood exposed to British culture and then nearly twenty years of travel in Britain. It's an exploration of why one American man loves Britain so much but also why Britain is such a wonderful place, worthy of loving unconditionally.

The narrative arc of the book answers this question by covering interesting topics related to Britain such as visiting for the first time, culture, stately home, tea, history, British TV, literature, specific places, and much more. Each chapter focuses on a specific topic, all building to the end where Jonathan reveals his 'Great British Dream.'

Come on a journey that will take you the length and breadth of Britain and its rich history.

ISBN: 978-0985477080

Available from all bookstores and direct from Anglotopia at http://adventuresinanglotopia.com

About Anglotopia.net

Anglotopia.net is the world's largest website for people who love Britain. Founded in 2007, it has grown to be the biggest community of passionate Anglophiles anywhere. With daily updates covering British Culture, History, and Travel - Anglotopia is the place to get your British Fix!

https://anglotopia.net
https://londontopia.net

Lightning Source UK Ltd.
Milton Keynes UK
UKHW051855091220
374777UK00004BA/419/J